# Autodesk Fusion 360 Basics Tutorial

## Tutorial Books

**For resource files contact us at:**

*Online.books999@gmail.com*

# Contents

## Contents

## Contents

# Contents

**Contents**

# INTRODUCTION

Autodesk Fusion 360 is a web-based modelling program. It is package of many modules delivering a great value to enterprises. It offers a set of tools, which are easy-to-use to design, document, simulate, and manufacture 3D models. Using this software, you can speed up the design process and reduce the product development costs.

This book provides a step-by-step approach for users to learn Autodesk Fusion 360. It is aimed for those with no previous experience with Fusion 360. The user will be guided from starting an Autodesk Fusion 360 session to creating parts, assemblies, and drawings. Each chapter has components explained with the help of real world models.

## Scope of this book

This book is written for students and engineers who are interested to learn Autodesk Fusion 360 for designing mechanical components and assemblies, and then create drawings.

This book provides a step-by-step approach for learning Autodesk Fusion 360. The topics include Getting Started with Autodesk Fusion 360, Basic Part Modeling, Creating Assemblies, Creating Drawings, Sketching, Additional Modeling Tools, Top-down assemblies, and Dimensions and Annotations.

**Chapter 1** introduces Autodesk Fusion 360. The user interface and terminology are discussed in this chapter.

**Chapter 2** takes you through the creation of your first Fusion 360 model. You create simple parts.

**Chapter 3** teaches you to create assemblies. It explains the Top-down and Bottom-up approaches for designing an assembly. You create an assembly using the Bottom-up approach.

**Chapter 4** teaches you to create drawings of the models created in the earlier chapters. You will also learn to place exploded views, and part list of an assembly.

**Chapter 5:** In this chapter, you will learn the sketching tools.

**Chapter 6:** In this chapter, you will learn additional modeling tools to create complex models.

**Chapter 7:** teaches you to create Top-down assemblies. It also introduces you create mechanisms by applying joints between the parts.

**Chapter 8:** teaches you to apply dimensions and annotations to a 2D drawing.

# Chapter 1: Getting Started with Fusion 360
## What is Fusion 360?

Autodesk Fusion 360 is a web and cloud based modeling application. Some of the key features of Fusion 360 are:

- Web and cloud based
- It supports Parametric and Direct Modeling
- It can be access from anywhere
- It helps you to collaborate with a team
- Simple user-interface
- It supports Free-form modeling
- It allows you to work on models created in other CAD applications
- It helps you to 3D print a model or generate toolpaths using CAM (Computer Aided Manufacturing)
- It helps you to perform Design study using the Simulation feature.
- It is updated very frequently unlike other CAD programs.

This tutorial book brings in the most commonly used features of Autodesk Fusion 360. In this chapter, you will learn some of the most commonly used features of Autodesk Fusion 360. In addition, you will learn about the user interface. In Autodesk Fusion 360, you create 3D parts and use them to create 2D drawings and 3D assemblies.

**Fusion 360 is Feature Based.** Features are shapes that are combined to build a part. You can modify these shapes individually.

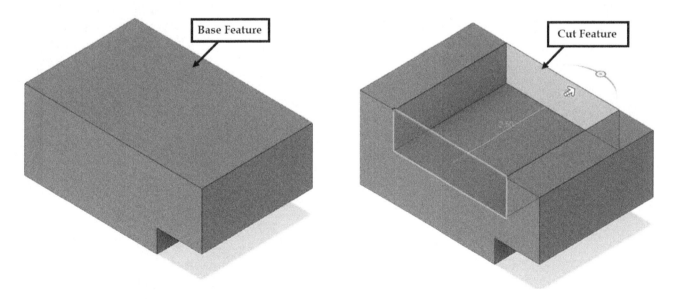

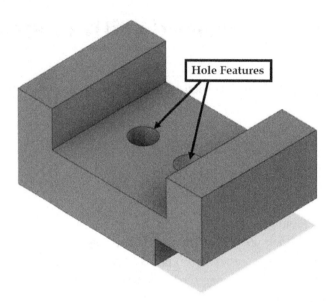

Hole Features

Most of the features are sketch-based. A sketch is a 2D profile and can be extruded, revolved, or swept along a path to create features.

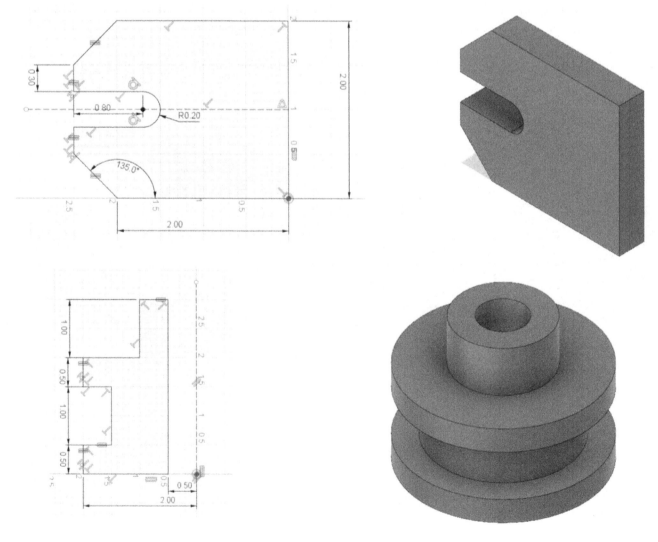

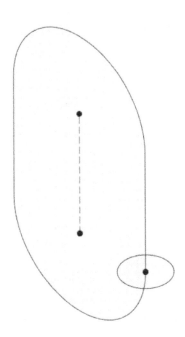
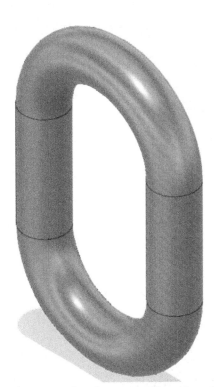

**Fusion 360 is parametric in nature**. You can specify standard parameters between the elements. Changing these parameters changes the size and shape of the part. For example, see the design of the body of a flange before and after modifying the parameters of its features.

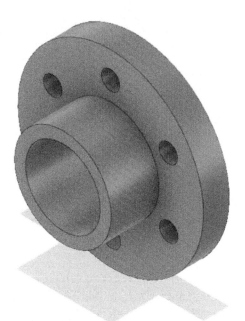
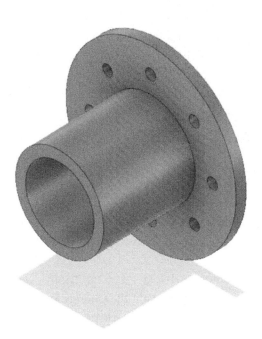

## Starting Autodesk Fusion 360

- Click the Windows icon on the taskbar.
- Click **A** > **Autodesk** > **Autodesk Fusion 360**.

Notice these important features of the Fusion 360 window.

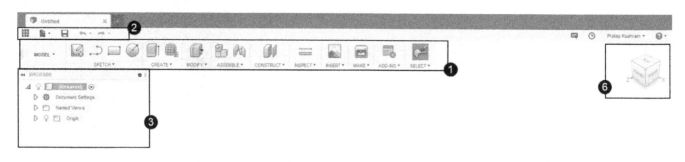

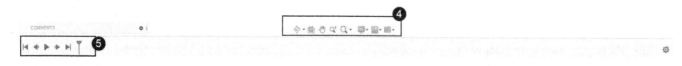

1.  Toolbar
2.  Application Bar
3.  Browser
4.  Navigation Bar
5.  Timeline
6.  ViewCube

# User Interface

Various components of the user interface are discussed next.

## Toolbar

Toolbar is located at the top of the window. The toolbar consists of various tools that are arranged on panels. You can select the required tool from a panel. By default, only few tools are displayed on the panels. You need to click the down arrow displayed on the panel to access more tools.

The set of tools displayed on the Toolbar depends on the Workspace which is currently active. You can change the workspace by using the **Change Workspace** drop-down displayed on the left side. Click on this drop-down and select the required workspace; a set of tools related to the selected workspace appear on the toolbar. The following sections explain the various workspaces available in Autodesk Fusion 360.

### The Model Workspace

The Toolbar in this workspace consists the tools to create sketches, 3D features, planes, assemblies, and so on.

## The Patch Workspace

The Toolbar in this workspace consists the tools to create and modify surfaces. The remaining tools on this Toolbar are same as that available in the Model Workspace.

## The Sheet Metal Workspace

The tools in this workspace are used to create sheet metal components.

## The Render Workspace

This Toolbar in this workspace contains the tools to create photo realistic images and videos.

## The Animation Workspace

The Toolbar in this workspace contains the tools to create the exploded views of an assembly. It also has the tools to create animation of an assembly.

## The Simulation Workspace

The Toolbar in this workspace contains the tools to perform engineering analysis of the components and assemblies.

## The CAM Workspace

The Toolbar in this workspace contains the tools to generate toolpaths for manufacturing operations such as milling, drilling, turning, and so on.

### The Drawing Workspace

In the Drawing workspace, you can create print-ready drawings of a 3D model. The Toolbar in this workspace contains the tools to create 2D drawings.

# File Menu

This appears when you click on the **File** icon located at the top left corner. This menu contains the options to create design, import design, print, export, manage, save, and so on.

# Application Bar

This is available at the top left of the window. It contains **File** menu, **Save**, **Undo**, and **Redo** icons. You can use the **Show Data Panel** (grid) icon to view the data panel.

# Browser

This is located at the left side of the window. It contains the **Document Settings**, **Named Views** and **Origin** folder. In addition to that, the bodies, components, sketches, and construction elements are grouped in folders. You can show or hide them using the bulb icons located next to them.

## Timeline

The Timeline is displayed at the bottom of the window. It displays the operations carried in an Autodesk Fusion 360 file. The Timeline is a key feature in making Fusion 360 a parametric modeling software. You can edit a sketch, feature, or construction element by simply double clicking on them in the Timeline. Click the Play button to view the sequence in which the model was created. Click and drag the Play Marker before a feature; the feature is suppressed.

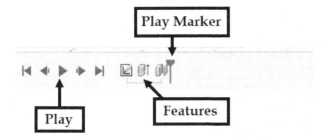

## Navigation Bar

This is located at the bottom of the graphics window above the Timeline. It contains the tools to zoom, rotate, pan, or look at a face of the model. You can also access the display settings, grid and snap settings, and viewport settings.

## View Cube

It is located at the top right corner of the graphics window. It is used to set the view orientation of the model.

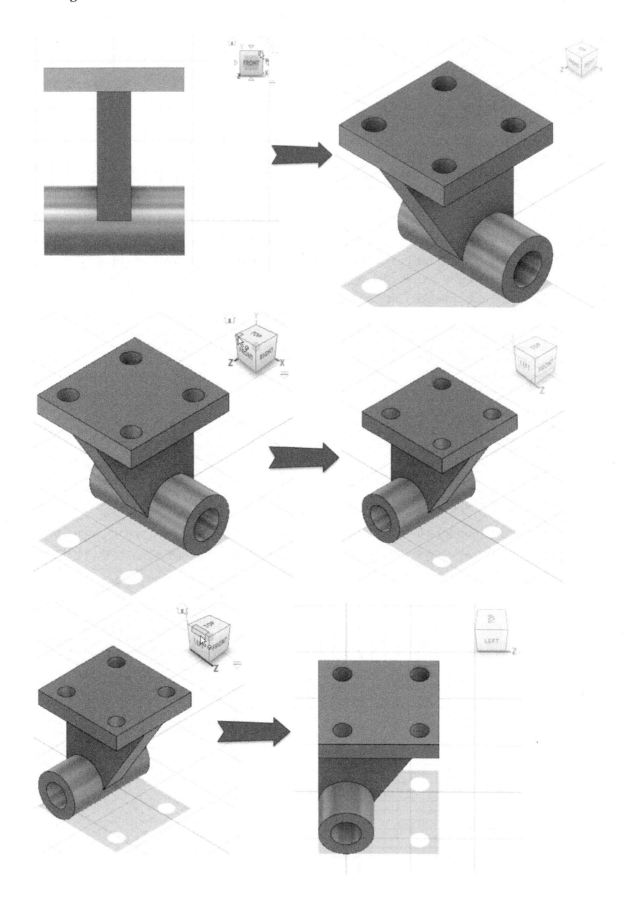

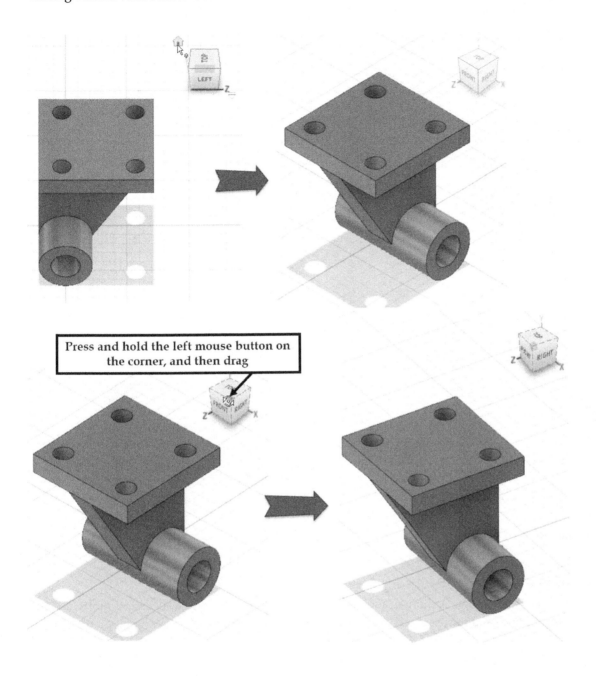

Press and hold the left mouse button on the corner, and then drag

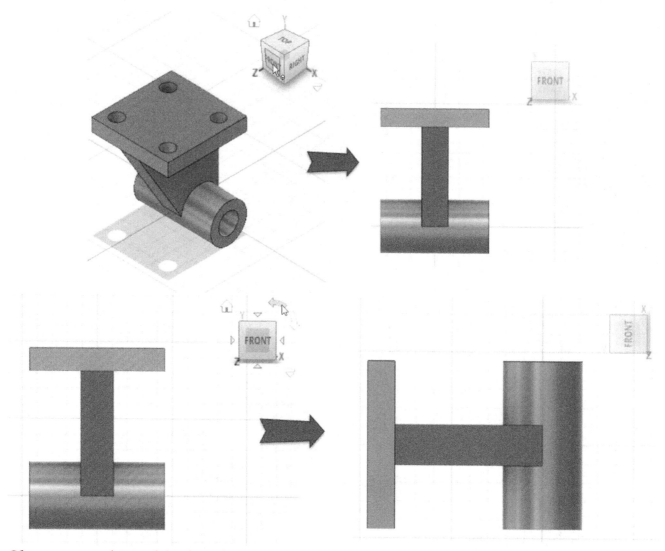

## Shortcut and Marking Menus

When you click the right mouse button, a shortcut menu along with a marking menu appears. A shortcut menu contains some important options and the list of the panels available on the toolbar. Place the pointer on the options to access the tools.

The marking menu contains some important tools in a radial fashion. It allows you to access the tools quickly.

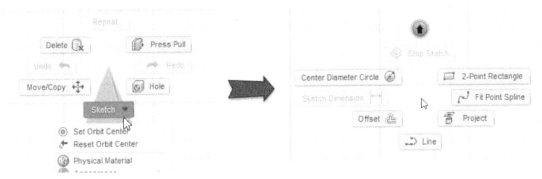

## Dialogs

When you activate any tool in Autodesk Fusion 360, the dialog related to it appears. It consists of various options, which help you to complete the operation. The following figure shows the components of the dialog.

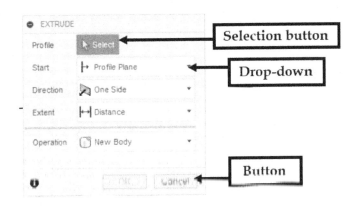

# Customizing the Toolbar

By default, not all tools are displayed on the Toolbar. However, you can display them on the panels of the Toolbar. To do this, click the down arrow displayed at the bottom of the panel. Next, place the pointer on the tool to be displayed on the panel. Click on the three dots displayed next to the tool, and then select Pin to Toolbar; the tool will be pinned to the Toolbar.

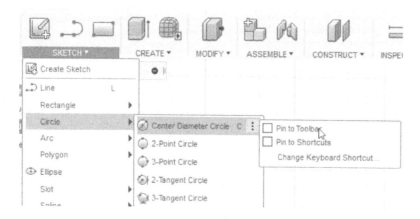

If you want to reset the panel, then right click on it and select **Reset Panel Customization**.

# The Quick Setup dialog

The **Quick Setup** dialog helps you to specify the default units and navigation controls. Also, you can start learning using the guided tutorials. This book uses **Inches** to create models so it is advised to set the **Default Units** to **in**. You can specify the navigation controls based on the CAD application you are familiar with.

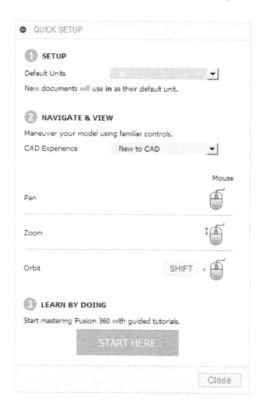

# Chapter 2: Part Modeling Basics

This chapter takes you through the creation of your first Fusion 360 model. You create simple parts:

In this chapter, you will:

- Create Sketches
- Create a base feature
- Add another feature to it
- Create revolved features
- Create cylindrical features
- Create box features
- Apply draft

## TUTORIAL 1

This tutorial takes you through the creation of your first Fusion 360 model. You will create the Disc of an Oldham coupling:

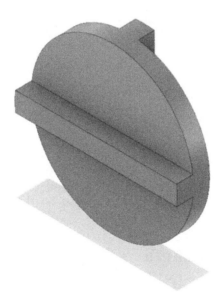

### Creating a New Project

1. Start **Autodesk Fusion 360** by double-clicking the **Autodesk Fusion 360** icon on your desktop.
2. To create a new project, click the **Show Data Panel** button located at the top left corner of the window.

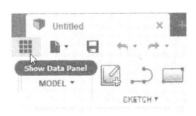

3. Click the **Leave Data Details** button.

4. Click the **New Project** button.

5. Type **Oldham Coupling** and press Enter.

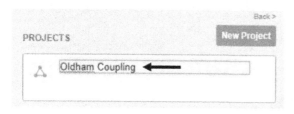

6. Click the **Close Data Panel** button.

7. On the **Quick Setup** dialog, select **Default Units > in**.
8. Select **CAD Experience > New to CAD**.
9. Click **Close** on the **Quick Setup** dialog.

## Starting a Sketch

1. To start a new sketch, click **Sketch > Create Sketch** on the Toolbar.

2. Click on the **XY Plane**. The sketch starts.

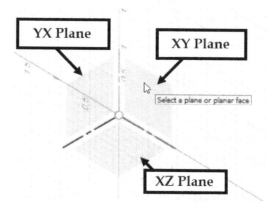

The first feature is an extruded feature from a sketched circular profile. You will begin by sketching the circle.

3. On the Toolbar, click **Sketch > Circle > Center Diameter Circle**.

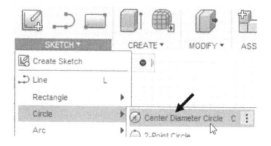

4. Move the cursor to the sketch origin located at the center of the graphics window, and then click on it.
5. Drag the cursor up to a random location, and then click to create a circle.

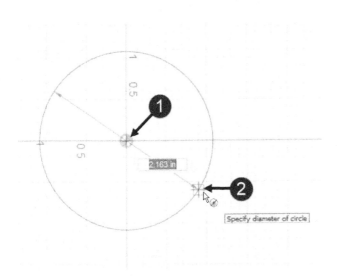

6.  Press **ESC** to deactivate the tool.

## Adding Dimensions

In this section, you will specify the size of the sketched circle by adding dimensions. As you add dimensions, the sketch can attain any one of the following states:

**Fully Constrained sketch:** In a fully constrained sketch, the positions of all the entities are fully described by dimensions, constraints, or both. In a fully constrained sketch, all the entities are black in color.

**Under Constrained sketch:** Additional dimensions, constraints, or both are needed to completely specify the geometry. In this state, you can drag under constrained sketch entities to modify the sketch. An under constrained sketch entity is in blue color.

If you add any more dimensions to a fully constrained sketch, a message box will appear showing that dimension over constraints the sketch. In addition, it prompts you to convert the dimension into a driven dimension. Click **Ok** to convert the unwanted dimension into a driven dimension.

1.  On the Toolbar, click **Sketch > Sketch Dimension**.

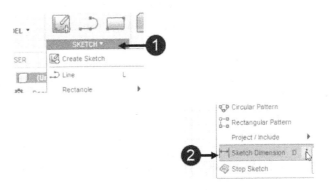

(or)

Right click in the graphics window, and then place the pointer on the **Sketch** option. Next, select **Sketch Dimension**.

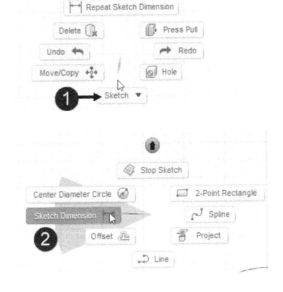

2.  Select the circle, move the pointer, and click; a value box appears.
3.  Enter **4** in the value box and press Enter.

4.  Press **Esc** to deactivate the **Sketch Dimension** tool.

You can also create dimensions while creating the sketch objects. To do this, enter the dimension values in the boxes displayed while sketching.

5.  To display the entire circle at full size and to center it in the graphics area, click **Zoom Window > Fit** on the **Navigation Bar**.

6.  Click **Stop Sketch** on the Toolbar.

7.  In the **Browser**, expand the **Named Views** node, and then click **HOME**.

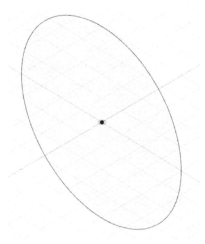

## Creating the Base Feature

The first feature in any part is called a base feature. You now create this feature by extruding the sketched circle.

1.  On the Toolbar, click **Create > Extrude**.

2.  Click in the region enclosed by the sketch.

3.  Type-in 0.4 in the **Distance** box available on the **Extrude** dialog.

4.  Select **Direction > One Side** on the **Extrude** dialog.

5.  Click **OK** on the **Extrude** dialog to create the extrusion.

Notice the new feature, **Extrude 1**, in the **Timeline**.

To magnify a model in the graphics area, you can use the zoom tools available on the **Navigation Bar**.

Click **Fit** to display the part full size in the current window.

Click **Zoom Window**, and then drag the pointer to create a rectangle; the area in the rectangle zooms to fill the window.

Click **Zoom**, and then drag the pointer. Dragging up zooms out; dragging down zooms in.

To display the part in different rendering modes, select the options in the **Visual Style** menu on the **Display Settings** drop-down of the Navigation Bar.

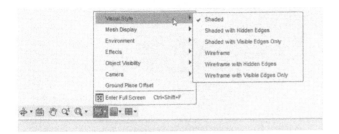

## Shaded with Visible Edges Only

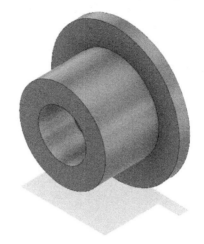

## Shaded

## Wireframe

## Shaded with Hidden Edges

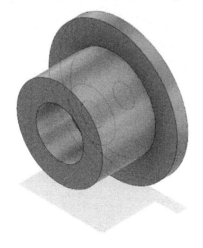

## Wireframe with Hidden Edges

## Wireframe with Visible Edges Only

The default display mode for parts and assemblies is **Shaded with Visible Edges Only**. You may change the display mode whenever you want.

## Adding an Extruded Feature

To create additional features on the part, you need to draw sketches on the model faces or planes, and then extrude them.

1. On the Toolbar, click **Sketch > Create Sketch**.
2. Click on the front face of the part.

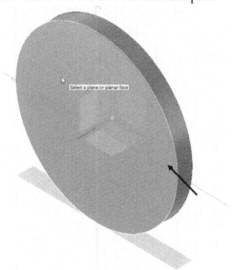

3. Click **Line** on the **Sketch** panel.

4. Click on the circular edge to specify the first point of the line.

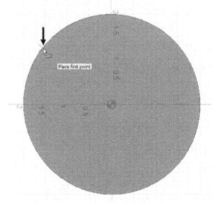

5. Move the cursor towards right.
6. Click on the other side of the circular edge; a line is drawn.

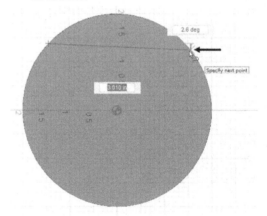

7. Draw another line below the previous line.

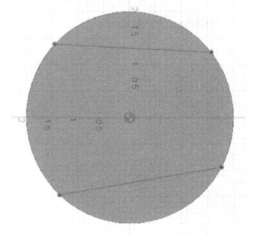

8. On the Sketch Palette, click **Horizontal/Vertical**.

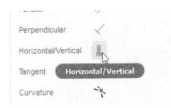

9. Select the two lines to make them horizontal.

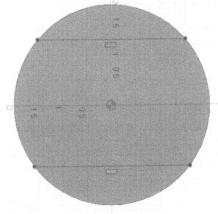

10. On the Sketch Palette, click **Constraints > Equal**
    = .
11. Select the two horizontal lines to make them
    equal.
12. Click **Sketch Dimension** on the **Sketch** panel of
    the Toolbar.
13. Select the two horizontal lines.
14. Move the cursor toward right and click to locate
    the dimension; the value box appears.
15. Enter **0.472** in the value box and press Enter.

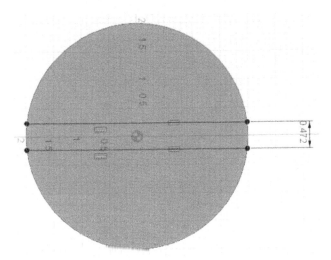

16. On the Toolbar, click **Create > Extrude**.

17. Click in the region bounded by the two
    horizontal lines.

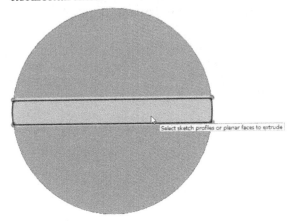

18. Enter **0.4** in the **Distance** box on the **Extrude**
    dialog.
19. On the **Extrude** dialog, click **Direction > One
    Side.**
20. Select **Operation > Join**, and then **OK** to create
    the extrusion.
21. Click on the **Home** icon next to the ViewCube.

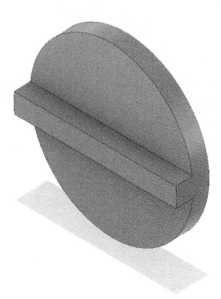

By default, the ground shadows and ambient
occlusion are displayed on the model. However, you

can turn off them by clicking Navigation Bar > **Display Settings** > **Effects** menu, and then unchecking the **Ground Shadows** and **Ambient Occlusion** options.

📝 *You can reuse the sketch of an already existing feature. To do this, expand the Sketches folder in the Browser, and then click on the blue bulb icon located next to the sketch. You will notice that the sketch is visible in the graphics window. You can also hide the sketch by clicking on the yellow bulb icon next to the sketch.*

## Adding another Extruded Feature

1. Click the **Free Orbit** button on the **Navigation Bar.**

2. Press and hold the left mouse button and drag the pointer to rotate the model.
3. Release the mouse button when the back face of the part is visible.

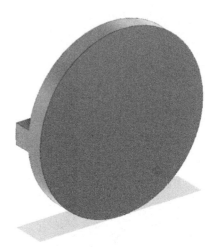

4. Right click and select **OK**.
5. Click **Create Sketch** on the **Sketch** panel of the Toolbar.
6. Click on the back face of the part.
7. Click **Line** ⌐⊃ on the **Create** panel.
8. Draw two lines, as shown below (refer to the **Adding an Extruded Feature** section to know how to draw lines). Make sure that the endpoints of the lines are coincident with the circular edge. Follow the next two steps, if they are not coincident.

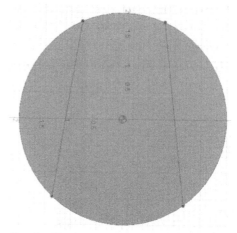

9. On the Sketch Palette, click **Constraints > Coincident** └ . Next, select the end point of the line and the circular edge.

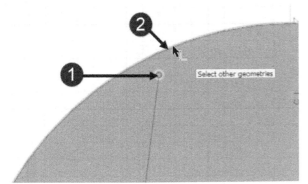

10. Likewise, make the other endpoints of the lines coincident with the circular edge.

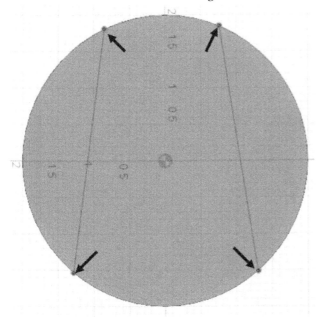

Skip the above two steps if the endpoints of the lines are coincident with the circular edge.

11. On the Sketch Palette, click **Constraints > Horizontal/Vertical** ⬚ .
12. Select the two lines to make them vertical.
13. On the Sketch Palette, click **Constraints > Equal** = .
14. Select the two vertical lines to make them equal.
15. On the Toolbar, click **Sketch > Sketch Dimension**.
16. Select the two vertical lines, move the pointer upward, and then click to position the dimension.
17. Type 0.472 in the value box, and then press Enter.

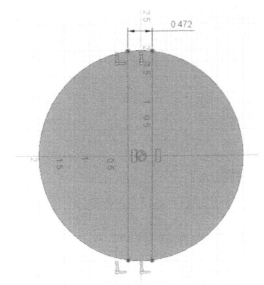

18. On the Toolbar, click **Create > Extrude**.
19. Click inside the region enclosed by two lines.
20. Type 0.4 in the **Distance** box on the **Extrude** dialog.
21. Select **Operation > Join** and click **OK**.

To move the part view, click **Pan** 🖐 on **Navigation Bar**, and then drag the part to move it in the graphics area.

22. Click on the **Home** icon next to the ViewCube

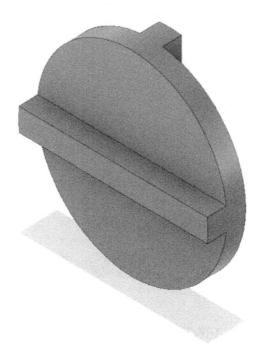

## Saving the Part

1.  Click **Save**  on the **Application bar**.
2.  On the **Save** window, type-in **Disc** in the **Name** box.
3.  Click the down arrow button next to the **Location** box.

4.  Select **Oldham Coupling** from the **Project** list.
5.  Click **Save** to save the file.
6.  Click the **Close** icon on the file tab.

# TUTORIAL 2

In this tutorial, you create a flange by performing the following operations:

- Creating a revolved feature
- Creating a cut features
- Adding fillets

## Sketching a Revolve Profile

You create the base feature of the flange by revolving a profile around a centerline.

1.  Click **Sketch > Create Sketch** on the Toolbar.
2.  Select the YZ plane.

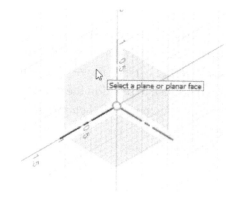

3.  Click **Line** 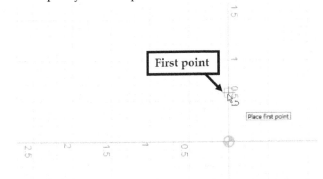 on the **Create** panel.

4.  Specify the first point of the line, as shown.

5.  Move the pointer horizontally toward left up to a scale value of 2.

6.  Click to create a horizontal line of 2 inches.

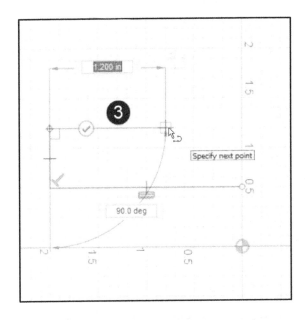

7.  Move the pointer vertically upward.

8.  Click when a value of 0.6 is displayed in the dimension attached to the line.

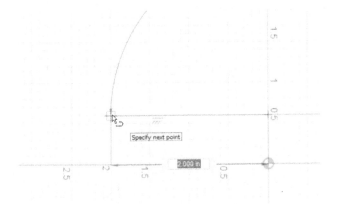

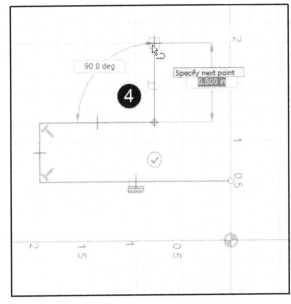

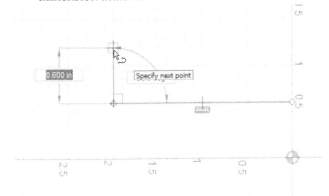

9.  Likewise, create the other lines in the sequence, as shown.

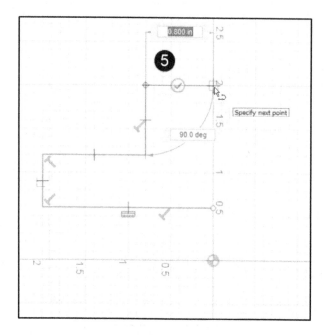

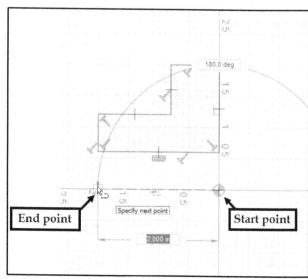

12. Right click and select **OK**.

13. On the Sketch Palette, click **Constraints >
    Coincident** ⌐ .

14. Select the vertical line and the origin point, as
    shown.

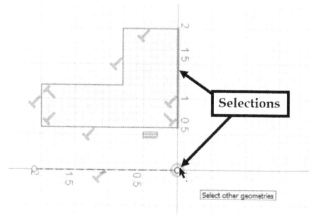

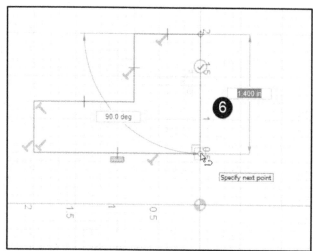

10. On the Sketch Palette, click **Options >
    Construction**.

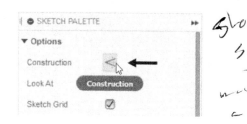

*Slotout
5X

must draw
a line, circle, rectangle.*

11. Create a construction line by specifying the start
    and end points, as shown below.

15. On the toolbar, click **Sketch > Sketch
    Dimension**.

16. Select the construction line and the horizontal
    line.

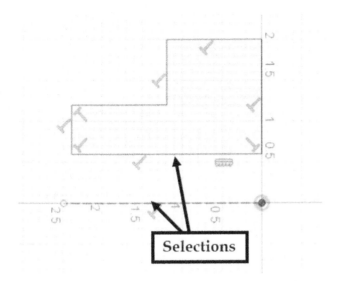

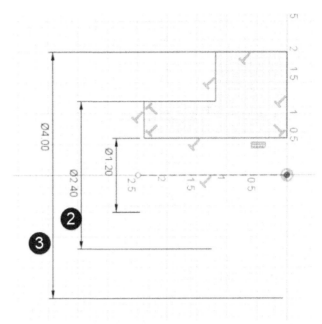

17. Right click and select **Diameter Dimension**.
18. Move the pointer horizontally toward left and click to place the dimension.
19. Type 1.2 in the value box.
20. Press Enter.

22. With the **Sketch Dimension** tool still active, select the horizontal line, as shown.

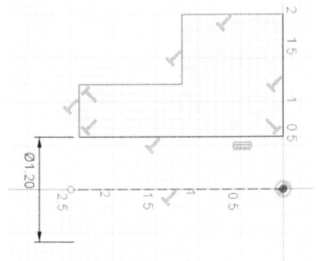

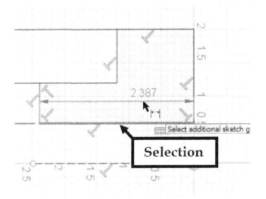

21. Likewise, create two more diameter dimensions, as shown.

23. Move the pointer upward, and click.
24. Type 2 in the value box and press Enter.

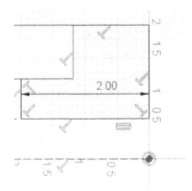

25. Select the top most horizontal line.

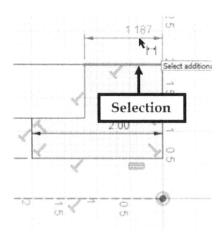

26. Move the pointer upward, and click.
27. Type 0.8 and press Enter.

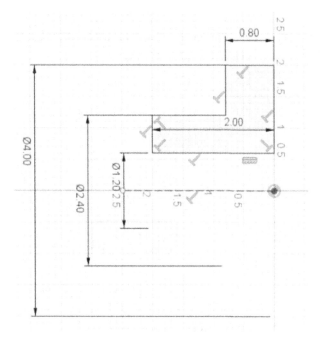

You can hide all the constraints by unchecking the **Show Constraints** option on the **Sketch Palette**. Likewise, you can display all the constraints by checking the **Show Constraints** option.

28. Right-click and select **Stop Sketch**.

## Creating the Revolved Feature

1. On the Toolbar, click **Create > Revolve** (or) right-click and select **Create > Revolve** from the Shortcut menu.

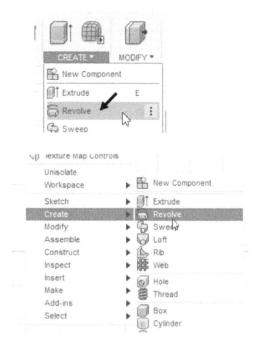

2. Click in the region enclosed by the sketch.
3. On the **Revolve** dialog, click the **Select** button next to the **Axis** option.
4. Select the construction line.

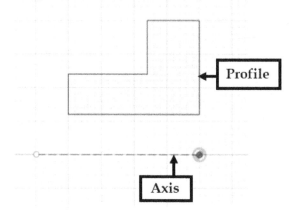

5. Set **Type** to **Full** on the **Revolve** dialog.

6. Click **OK** to create the revolved feature.
7. Click on the **Home** icon next to the ViewCube.

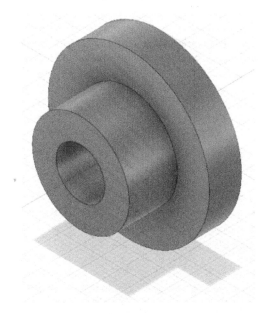

## Creating the Cut feature

1. On the Navigation Bar, click **Orbit > Constrained Orbit**.

Notice a grey circle with quadrant lines is displayed, as shown.

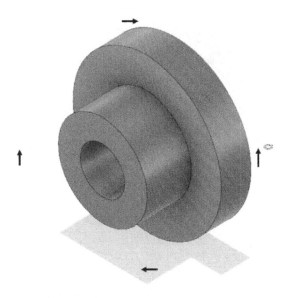

2. Place the pointer on the right horizontal line.
3. Press and hold the left mouse button and drag the mouse toward left.

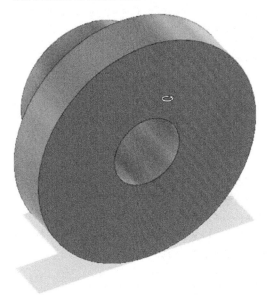

4. Release the left mouse button when the back face of the model is visible.
5. Right click and select **OK**.
6. On the Toolbar, click **Sketch > Create Sketch** .
7. Click the back face of the part; the sketch starts.

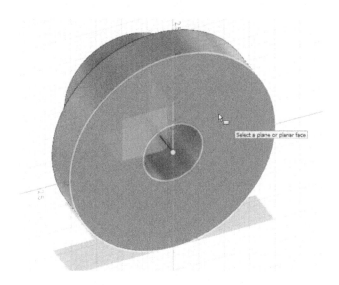

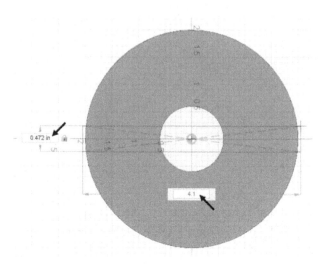

8. On the Toolbar, click **Sketch > Rectangle > Center Rectangle**.

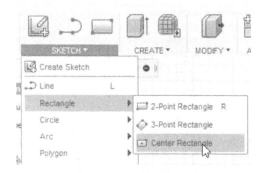

9. Select the origin to define the center point.
10. Move the cursor diagonally toward right.
11. Enter .472 in the vertical dimension box.
12. Press Tab key and enter 4.1 in the horizontal dimension box. Press Enter twice.

13. Click the **Stop Sketch** button located at the bottom of the Sketch Palette.
14. Press the Ctrl key and click inside the sketch regions, as shown.

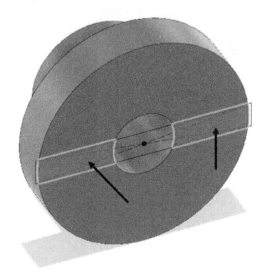

15. Right click and select **Extrude**; the **Extrude** dialog appears.
16. Select **Operation > Cut** from the **Extrude** dialog.
17. Enter -0.4 in the **Distance** box.
18. Click **OK** to create the cut feature.

## Creating another Cut feature

1. Click the **Home** icon located at the top left corner of the ViewCube.

2. Create a sketch on the front face of the base feature.

   - On the Toolbar, click **Sketch > Create Sketch**.
   - Select the front face of the model.

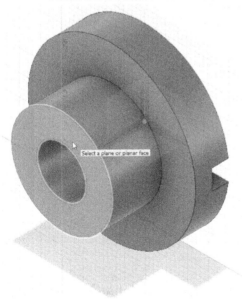

   - On the Toolbar, click **Sketch > Line**.

- Click on the inner circular edge to define the start point, as shown.
- Move the pointer horizontally toward right, and then click. Notice that the Horizontal constraint is applied to the line.
- Move the pointer vertically downward, and then click. Notice that the Vertical constraint is applied.
- Move the pointer toward left and click on the inner circular edge.

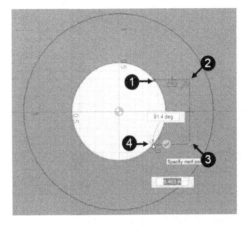

- Right click and select **OK**.
- On the Sketch Palette, click **Constraints > Horizontal/Vertical**.
- Select the third line to make it horizontal.

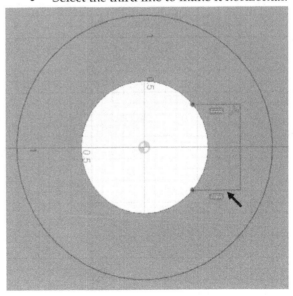

- On the Sketch Palette, click **Constraints > Equal.**

- Select the two horizontal lines to make them equal in length.
- Ensure that the endpoints of the horizontal lines coincide with the inner circular edge.
- Apply dimension of 0.236 to the vertical line.
- Apply dimension of 0.118 to horizontal line.
- Press Esc.

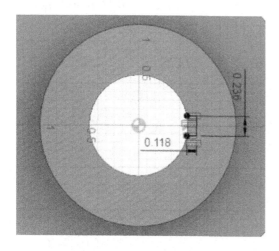

3. Click **Stop Sketch** on the Toolbar.
4. Click **Extrude** on the **Create** panel of the Toolbar.
5. Click in the region enclosed by the three lines and circular edge.

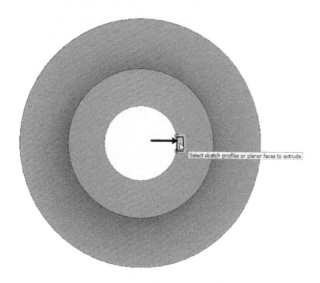

6. Click the **Home** icon next to the ViewCube.
7. On the **Extrude** dialog, select **All** from the **Extent** drop-down.

8. Select **Operation > Cut** from the **Extrude** dialog.
9. Click the **Flip** icon on the **Extrude** dialog, if the arrow on the sketch points towards front.

10. Click **OK** to create the cut feature.

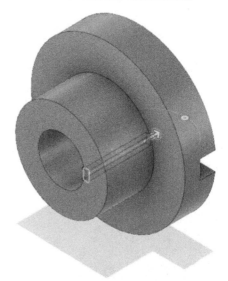

## Adding a Fillet

1. On the Toolbar, click **Modify > Fillet** (or) right-click and select **Modify > Fillet**.

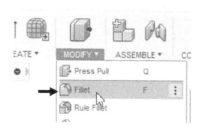

2. Click on the inner circular edge.

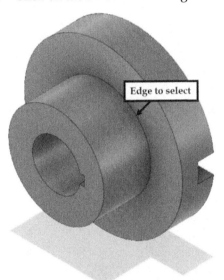

3. On the **Fillet** dialog, select Type > **Constant Radius**.
4. Type 0.2 in the **Radius** box.

5. Click **OK** to add the fillet.

## Saving the Part

1. Click **Save** 🖫 on the **Application bar**.
2. On the **Save** window, type-in **Flange** in the **Name** box.
3. Click the down arrow button next to ``the **Location** box.
4. Select **Oldham Coupling** from the **Project** list.
5. Click **Save** to save the file.
6. Click the **Close** icon on the file tab.

# TUTORIAL 3

In this tutorial, you create the Shaft by performing the following operations:

- Creating a cylindrical feature
- Creating a cut feature

## Creating the Cylindrical Feature

1. On the Toolbar, click **Create > Cylinder**.

2. Click on the XY plane to select it; the sketch starts.
3. Click at the origin and move the cursor outward.
4. Enter 1.2 in the box attached to the circle.

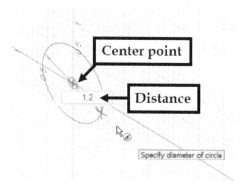

5. Press Enter key twice; the **Cylinder** dialog appears.
6. Enter **4** in the **Height** box.

7. Click **OK** to create the cylinder.

## Creating Cut feature

1. Create a sketch on the front face of the base feature.
   - On the Toolbar, click **Sketch > Create Sketch** .
   - Select the front face of the cylinder.
   - On the Toolbar, click **Sketch > Line**.
   - Specify the points of the lines in the sequence, as shown.

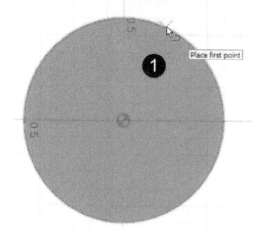

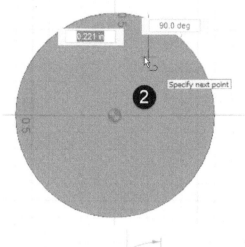

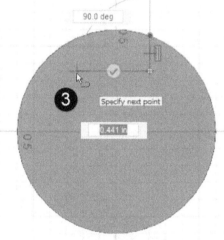

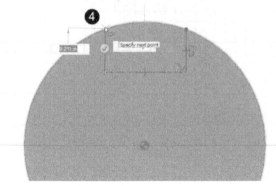

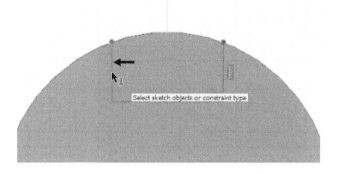

- On the Sketch palette, click **Constraints > Equal**.
- Click on the two vertical lines.
- On the Toolbar, click **Sketch > Sketch Dimension**.
- Add dimensions to the sketch.

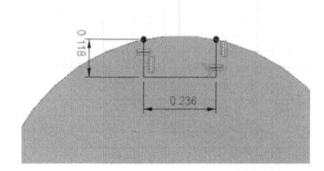

2. Click **Stop Sketch** on the **Sketch** palette.
3. Click the **Home** icon next to the ViewCube.
4. Click the **Extrude** button on the **Create** panel.
5. Click in the region enclosed by the sketch.
6. Click **Operation > Cut** on the **Extrude** dialog.
7. Set **Distance** to **-2.165**.
8. Click **OK** to create the cut feature.

- Right click and select **OK**.
- Make sure that the **Coincident** constraint is applied between the end points of the vertical lines and the circular edge.
- On the **Sketch** palette, click **Constraints > Horizontal/Vertical**.
- Click on the left vertical line.

## Saving the Part

1. Click **Save** 💾 on the **Application bar**.
2. On the **Save** window, type-in **Shaft** in the **Name** box.
3. Click the down arrow button next to the **Location** box.
4. Select **Oldham Coupling** from the **Project** list.
5. Click **Save** to save the file.
6. Click the **Close** icon on the file tab.

## TUTORIAL 4

In this tutorial, you create a Key by performing the following:

- Creating a Box feature
- Applying draft

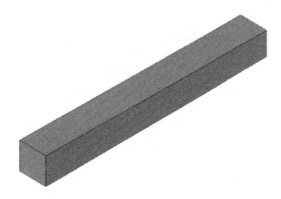

## Creating a Box

1. On the Toolbar, **Create > Box**.

2. Select the XY plane.
3. Create the sketch, as shown in figure.

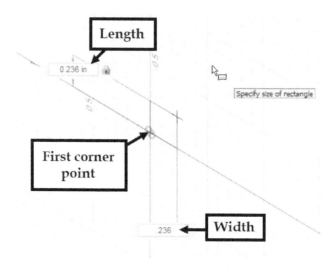

4. Press ENTER.
5. Enter 2 in the **Height** box.
6. Click **OK** to create the box.

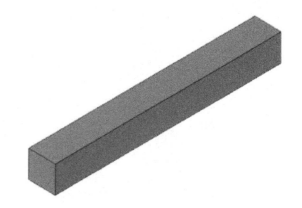

## Applying Draft

1. On the Toolbar, click **Modify > Draft**.

2. Click the **Select** button next to the **Plane** option.

3. Select the front face as the parting plane.

Select parting plane

4. Select the top face as the face to be draft.

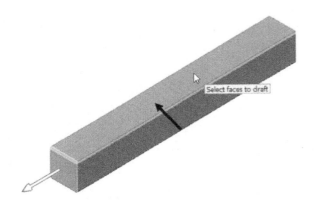

Select faces to draft

5. Set **Draft Angle** to **1**.
6. Click the **Flip Direction** button on the **Draft** dialog.

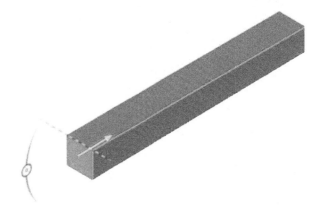

7. Click **OK** to create the draft.

## Saving the Part

1. Click **Save** 🖫 on the **Application bar**.
2. On the **Save** window, type-in **Key** in the **Name** box.
3. Click **Save** to save the file.
4. Click the **Close** icon on the file tab.

# Chapter 3: Assembly Basics

In this chapter, you will:

- Add Components to assembly
- Fix the components together
- Create exploded view of the assembly

## TUTORIAL 1

This tutorial takes you through the creation of your first assembly. You create the Oldham coupling assembly:

| PARTS LIST | | |
|---|---|---|
| ITEM | PART NUMBER | QTY |
| 1 | Disc | 1 |
| 2 | Flange | 2 |
| 3 | Shaft | 2 |
| 4 | Key | 2 |

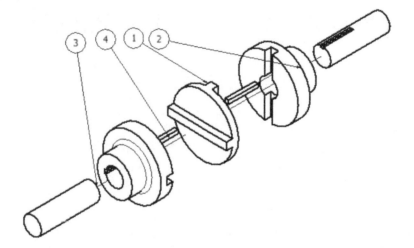

There are two ways of creating any assembly model.

- Top-Down Approach
- Bottom-Up Approach

### Top-Down Approach
The assembly file is created first and components are created in that file.

### Bottom-Up Approach
The components are created first, and then added to the assembly file. In this tutorial, you will create the assembly using this approach.

## Inserting the Base Component
You need to save the design before inserting a component into it.

1. On the Application Bar, click the **Save** icon.
2. Type **Flange assembly** in the **Name** box on the **Save** dialog.
3. Click **Save**.
4. To insert the base component, click the **Show Data Panel** icon.

5. Click the **Leave Data Details** button.

6. Double-click on the Oldham Coupling project to make it active.
7. Right click on the Flange file in the Data panel, and then select **Insert into Current Design**.

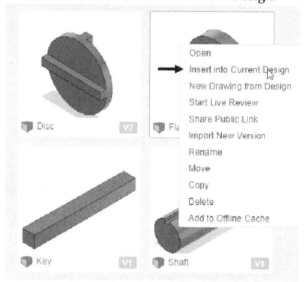

8. Click **OK** on the **Move/Copy** dialog.
9. In the Browser, right click on the Flange, and then select **Ground**; the component is fixed and it is unmovable.

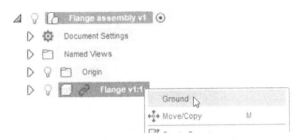

# Adding the second component

1. To insert the second component, right-click on the Shaft in the Data panel, and then select **Insert into Current Design**.

2. Click **OK** on the **Move/Copy** dialog.
3. Close the **Data** panel.

# Assembling the Components

After inserting the components into the design, you need to assemble them together. Autodesk Fusion 360 provides you with the **Joint** tool to assemble the components and establish real-life movements between them.

1. On the Toolbar, click **Assembly > Joint**.

2. On the **Joint** dialog, select **Type > Rigid**.
3. Select the circular edge of the shaft, as shown.

4. Select the circular edge on the back side of the flange, as shown.

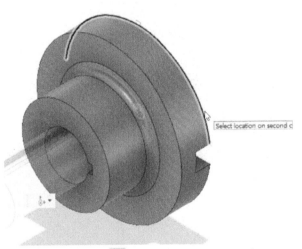

5. Click the **Flip** icon on the **Joint** dialog.
6. Type **270** in the **Angle** box; the shaft is rotated by the specified angle.
7. Type -0.4 in the **Offset Z** box; the shaft is offset by the specified distance. Also, the flat face of the shaft is aligned with the planar face of the cut feature, as shown.

8.  Click **OK** on the **Joint** dialog.

## Adding the Third Component

1.  Click the **Show Data Panel** icon on the top left corner of the window.
2.  On the **Data** panel, right click on Key and select **Insert into Current Design**.
3.  Click and drag the arrow pointing toward right.

4.  Click **OK** on the **Move/Copy** dialog.
5.  Close the **Data** panel.
6.  On the Toolbar, click **Assemble > Joint**.
7.  On the **Joint** dialog, select **Type > Rigid**.
8.  Move the pointer onto the side face of the key.
9.  Press and hold the left mouse button to display a dialog.
10. Move the pointer over the faces displayed on the dialog until the bottom face of the key is highlighted.
11. Select the highlighted face from the dialog.

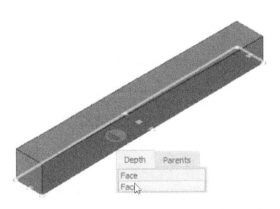

12. Select the midpoint of the lower front edge of the key to define the pivot point.

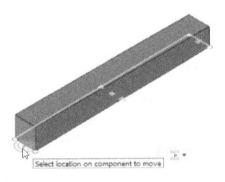

13. Select the flat face of the cut feature of the shaft.

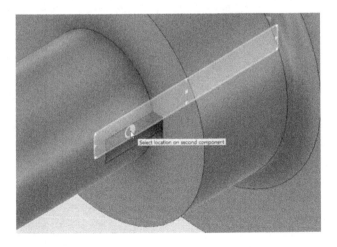

14. Select the midpoint of the edge, as shown.

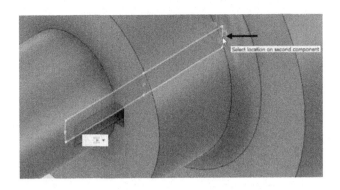

15. On the **Joint** dialog, type **180** in the **Angle** box.
16. Click **OK**.

The key is inserted in the cut feature of the shaft.

17. Click **Save** on the **Application bar**.
18. Click **OK** on the **Add Version Description** dialog.
19. Click the **Close** icon on the file tab.

## Creating the Main Assembly

When you close a file, a new file is opened automatically.

1. On the Application Bar, click the **Save** icon.
2. Type **Oldham Coupling** in the **Name** box on the **Save** dialog.
3. Click **Save**.
4. To insert the base component, click the **Show Data Panel** icon.
5. Right click on the Disc file in the **Data** panel, and then select **Insert into Current Design**.
6. Click **OK** on the **Move/Copy** dialog.
7. In the Browser, right click on Disc, and then select **Ground**.

## Placing the Sub-assembly

1. To insert the sub-assembly, right click on the Flange assembly file in the **Data** panel, and then select **Insert into Current Design**; the Flange assembly is inserted into the design.

2. Click and drag the arrow displayed in the Z-direction; the flange assembly is moved.

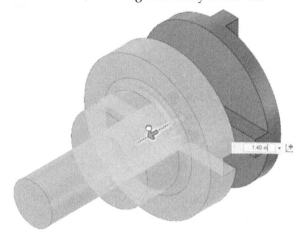

3. Click **OK** on the **Move/Copy** dialog.

## Adding Joints

1. Click **Joint** on the **Assemble** panel.
2. Select **Type > Rigid** on the **Joint** dialog.
3. Place the pointer on the flat face of the cut feature.
4. Click on the flat face when the pivot point is displayed on the midpoint of the edge, as shown.

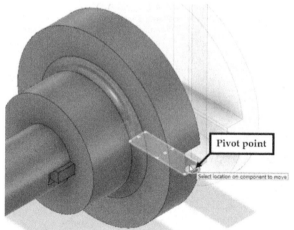

The midpoint of the edge is selected as the pivot point.

5. Press and hold the left mouse button on the front face of the Disc; a dialog pops up.
6. Select the bottom face of the extruded feature from the dialog.

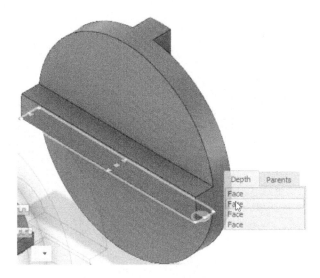

7. Select the midpoint of the edge to define the pivot point, as shown.

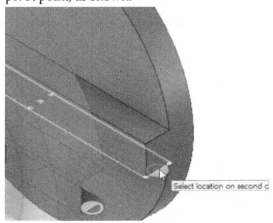

8. Click **OK**.

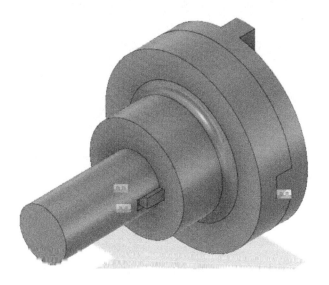

## Placing the second instance of the Sub-assembly

1. In the Browser, right click on the Flange assembly, and then select **Copy**.
2. Right click in the graphics window, and then select **Paste**.
3. Click and drag the arrow pointing in the Z-direction, as shown.

4. Click on the Rotate handle displayed along the Y-axis.
5. Type 180 in the **Angle** box displayed in the graphics window, and then press Enter.

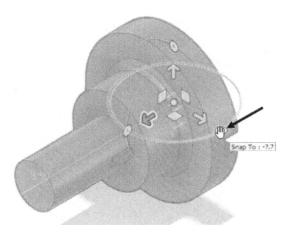

6. Click on the Rotate handle displayed along the Z-axis.
7. Type 90 in the **Angle** box displayed in the graphics window, and then press Enter.

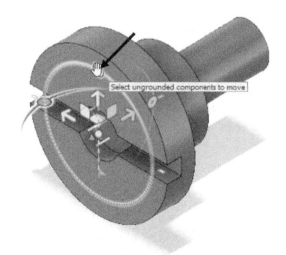

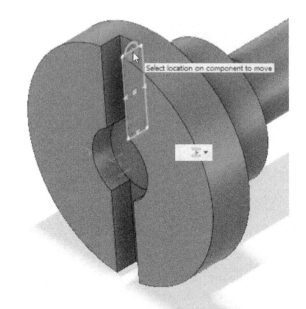

8. Right click and select **OK**.

9. Click **Joint** on the **Assemble** panel.

10. Select **Type > Rigid** on the **Joint** dialog.

11. Press and hold the left mouse button on the upper portion of the front face of the flange assembly.

12. Select the side face of the cut feature, as shown.

14. Place the pointer on the top portion of the side face of the Disc.

15. Click when the pivot point appears on the midpoint of the top edge.

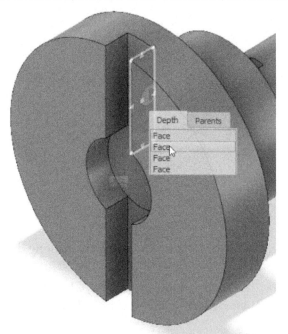

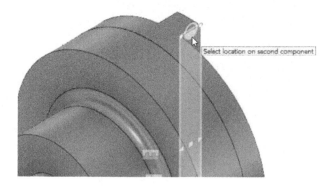

16. Click **OK**.

13. Select the midpoint of the top edge to define the pivot point.

17. Click **Save** on the Application Bar.

18. Click **OK**.

# TUTORIAL 2

In this tutorial, you create the exploded view of the assembly:

## Starting a New Animation

1. Open the **Oldham Coupling** file, if not already opened.

2. On the Toolbar, click **Change Workspace** drop-down > **ANIMATION**.

The ANIMATION Workspace appears, as shown.

## Creating a Storyboard Animation

1. In the ANIMATION TIMELINE, right-click on **Storyboard1 tab** and select **Rename**.

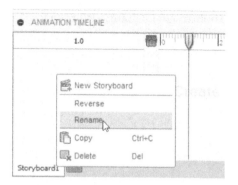

2. Type **Explosion** and press **Enter**.

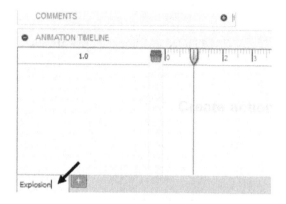

Before creating an exploded view, you need to take a look at the Storyboard displayed at the bottom of the window. The Storyboard has the Scratch Zone located at the left side of the timeline.

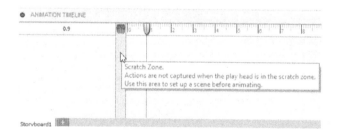

## Auto Explode Components

1. In the Browser, click the **Components** node to select all the components of the assembly.

2. Click the **Auto Explode All Levels** button on the **Transform** panel of the Toolbar. A mini toolbar appears, as shown.

3. Adjust the explosion distance using the **Explosion Scale** dragger.
4. Click the **Trail Line Visibility** icon on the Mini toolbar.

5. Click **OK** ✓ on the mini toolbar to explode the components.

6. Select **Components** from the Browser.
7. On the Toolbar, click **Transform > Restore Home**.

The components are restored to their original position.

8. Click the **Full screen** icon located at the bottom of the storyboard; the model is displayed in the full screen window.

9. Click the **Play Current Storyboard** icon; the explosion is played.

10. Click the Normal Mode icon located at the bottom right corner.

## Publishing the Animation Video

1. On the Toolbar, click **Publish** panel > **Publish Video** .
2. On the **Video Options** dialog, select **Current Storyboard** option from the **Video Scope** drop-down.
3. On the **Video Options** dialog, select **Current Document Window Size** option from the **Video Resolution** section.
4. Click **OK**.

5. Check the Save to Computer option, and then click the folder icon.
6. Specify the file location on the computer.
7. Type Auto_explode in the **File name** box.
8. Set the **Save as type** to **AVI (*.avi)**.
9. Click **Save** twice.

# Tutorial 3

In this tutorial, you will explode the components of the assembly manually.

## Exploding the Components Manually

1. On the Toolbar, click **Storyboard** > **New Storyboard**.

2. On the **New Storyboard** dialog, select **Storyboard Type** > **Clean**.
3. Click **OK**.
4. Click the Minimize icon on the ANIMATION TIMELINE.

5. On the Toolbar, click **Transform** > **Manual Explode**.

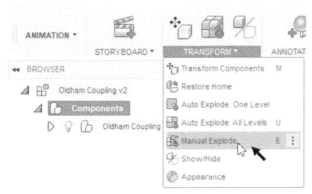

6. Select the Shaft from the graphics window, as shown.
7. Click on the arrow pointing in the Z-axis, as shown.

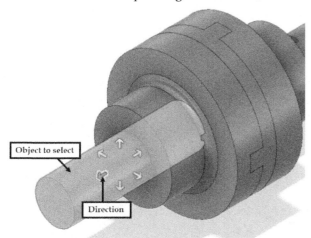

8. Click the **Trail Line Visibility** icon on the mini toolbar.
9. Click and drag the **Explosion Scale** dragger and position it at the middle.
10. Click **OK**.
11. Click **Fit** on the **Navigation Bar**.

12. Likewise, explode the remaining components, as shown.

13. Click the Maximize icon on the ANIMATION TIMELINE.

Notice that the actions are recorded on the timeline.

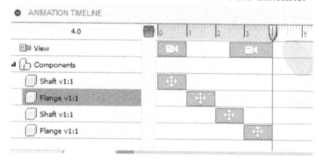

Right click on anyone of the actions and notice the different options in the Shortcut menu.

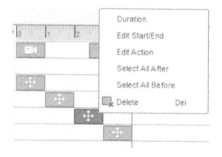

You can perform various operations on an action such as changing its duration, editing, changing the start/end, or deleting.

14. Publish the animation to a video file (refer to Publishing the Animation Video section in Tutorial 2).
15. Save and close the Assembly file.

# Chapter 4: Creating Drawings

In this chapter, you will generate 2D drawings of the parts and assemblies.

In this chapter, you will:

- Insert standard views of a part model
- Add dimensions and annotations
- Insert exploded view of the assembly
- Insert a bill of materials of the assembly
- Apply balloons to the assembly view

## TUTORIAL 1

In this tutorial, you will create the drawing of Flange created in the second chapter.

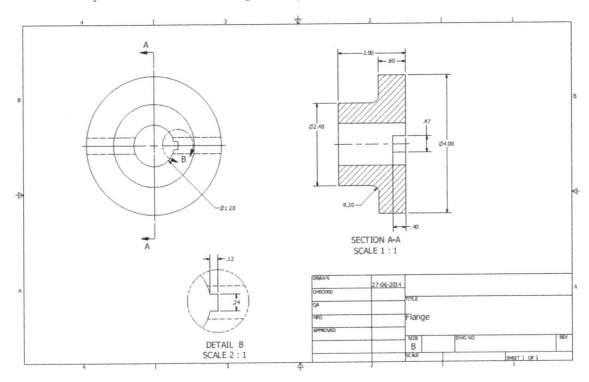

### Starting a New Drawing File

1. Click on the **Show Data Panel** icon on the Application Bar.
2. On the **Data** panel, double-click on the **Oldham Coupling** file to open it.
3. Close the **Data** panel.

4. To start a new drawing, click **File > New Drawing > From Design** on the Application Bar.

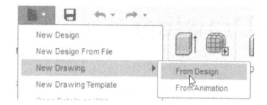

5. On the **Create Drawing** dialog, uncheck the **Full Assembly** option.

6. Select the Flange from the assembly.
7. Select **Template > From Scratch**.
8. Select **Standard > ASME**.
9. Select **Units > in**.
10. Select **Sheet Size > B (17in x 11in)**.
11. Click **OK**.

The Drawing environment appears, as shown.

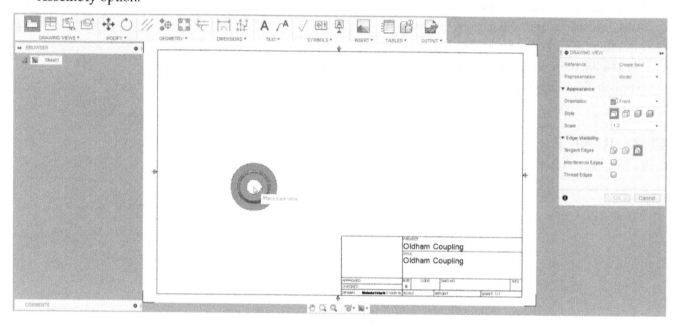

## Generating the Base View

The **Base View** tool is activated immediately after starting a new drawing.

1. On the **Drawing View** dialog, select **Orientation > Front**.
2. On the **Drawing View** dialog, set the **Style** to **Visible and Hidden Edges** .
3. Set **Scale** to **1:1**.
4. Set **Tangent Edges** to **Off** .
5. Place the drawing view at the left side on the drawing sheet, as shown.
6. Click **OK** on the dialog.

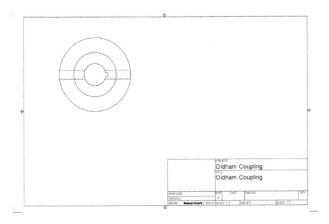

## Generating the Section View

1. To create the section view, click **Drawing Views > Section View** on the Toolbar.

2. Select the base view.
3. Place the cursor on the center point of the view, as shown.

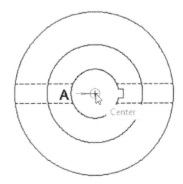

4. Move the pointer upward and notice the dotted line.

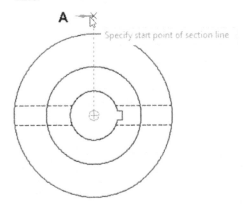

5. Click on the dotted line and move the cursor vertically downwards.
6. Click outside the bottom portion of the view, as shown.

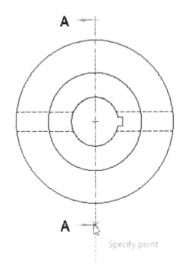

7. Right-click and select **Continue**.

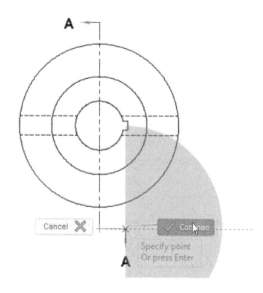

2. Select the base view.
3. On the **Drawing View** dialog, set **Style** to **From Parent**.
4. Select **Scale > 2:1**.
5. Specify the center point and boundary point of the detail view, as shown in figure.

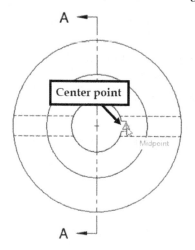

8. Move the cursor toward right and click to place the section view.

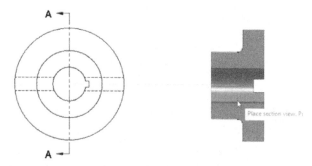

9. Click **OK** on the **Drawing View** dialog.

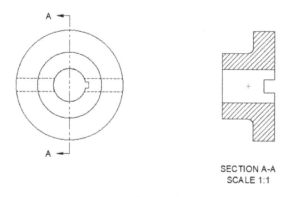

SECTION A-A
SCALE 1:1

## Creating the Detailed View

Now, you have to create the detailed view of the keyway, which is displayed, in the front view.

1. To create the detailed view, click **Drawing Views > Detail View** on the Toolbar.

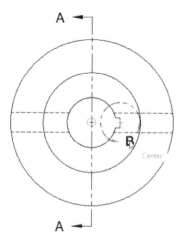

6. Place the detail view below the base view.
7. Click **OK**.

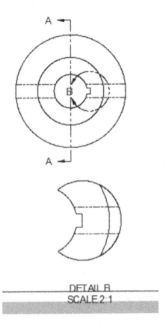

Notice that the label is placed outside the sheet. You need to move it inside.

8. Click on the label, and then select the square point displayed on it.

9. Move the pointer upward and click to place the label, as shown.

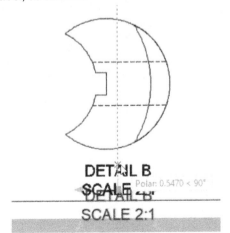

## Creating Centermarks and Centerlines

1. To create a center mark, click **Geometry > Center Mark** on the Toolbar.

2. Click on the outer circle of the base view.

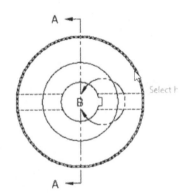

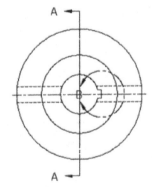

3. To create a centerline, click **Geometry > Centerline** on the Toolbar.

4. Click on the inner horizontal edges of the section view.

53

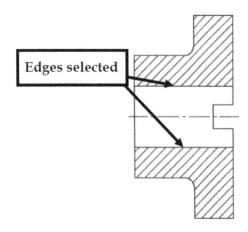

## Adding Dimensions

Now, you will add dimensions to the drawing.

1. To add dimensions, click **Dimensions > Dimension** on the Toolbar.

2. Zoom to the section view and select the corner points on the left side, as shown; a dimension is attached to the pointer.

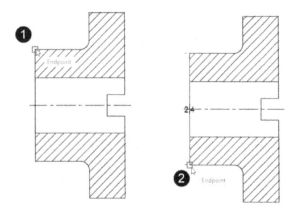

3. Move the pointer toward left and notice that the dimension is snapped to distance.

4. Click to position the dimension at the snapped point.

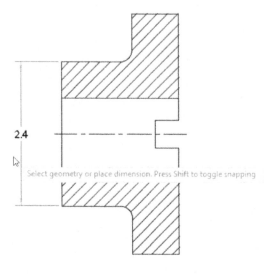

5. Likewise, add other linear dimensions to the section view.

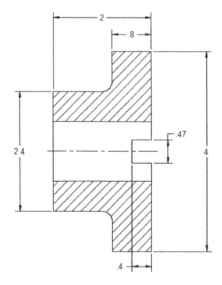

6. Press Esc to deactivate the **Dimension** tool.

7. Double-click on the 2.4 linear dimension.

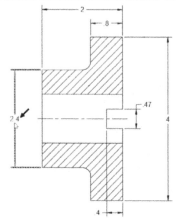

8. Click before the dimension value.

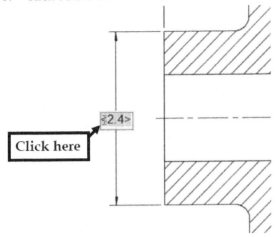

9. Press the **Space** key on your keyboard.
10. On the **Dimension** dialog, select **Insert symbol** drop-down > **Diameter**.
11. Click **Close** on the dialog.

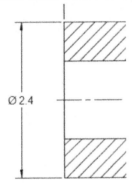

12. Likewise, add the diameter symbol to linear dimension with the value of 4.

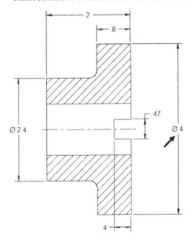

13. On the Toolbar, click **Dimensions > Radius Dimension**.

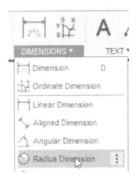

14. Select the fillet on the section view, as shown.
15. Move the pointer diagonally downward, and then click to position the dimension.

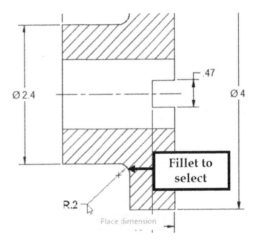

16. Right click and select **OK**.

Next, you need to add the diameter dimension.

17. Click **Dimensions > Diameter Dimension** on the Toolbar.

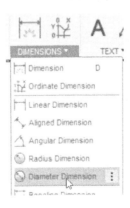

18. Select the center hole on the base view.

19. Place the dimension, as shown in figure.

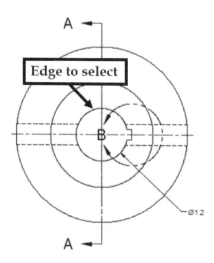

20. Right click and select **OK**.
21. Create the dimensions on the detail view, as shown in figure.

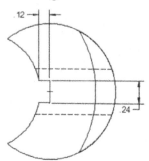

DETAIL B
SCALE 2:1

22. Click the **Annotation Settings** drop-down at the bottom, and select **Display Leading Zeroes**.

Zero is added before the dimension values.

## Populating the Title Block

1. To populate the title block, double-click on it; the **Title Block** dialog appears.
2. On the **Title Block** dialog, enter the data in the data fields.
3. Click the **Insert Image** icon in the **Logo** section, and then select the company logo from your computer.
4. Specify the location of the logo on the Title block.
5. Click **OK**.

## Saving the Drawing

1. Click **Save** on the **Application Bar**.
2. Type-in **Flange** in the **Name** box.
3. Click **Save** to save the file.
4. Click **Close** on the file tab.

# TUTORIAL 2

In this tutorial, you will create the drawing of the Oldham coupling assembly created in the previous chapter.

## Creating a New Drawing File

1. To start a new drawing, click **File > New Drawing > From Design** on the Application Bar.

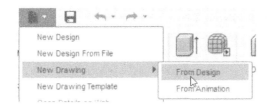

2. On the **Create Drawing** dialog, check the **Full Assembly** option.
3. Select **Template > From Scratch**.
4. Select **Standard > ASME**.
5. Select **Units > in**.
6. Select **Sheet Size > B (17in x 11in)**.
7. Click **OK**.

## Generating Base View

The **Base View** tool is activated immediately after starting a new drawing.

1. On the **Drawing View** dialog, select **Orientation > HOME**.
2. On the **Drawing View** dialog, set the **Style** to Visible Edges ⬚ .
3. Set **Scale** to **1:2**.
4. Set **Tangent Edges** to **Full Length** ⬚ .
5. Place the drawing view at the left side on the drawing sheet, as shown.

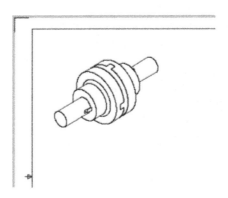

6. Click **OK** on the dialog.

## Generating the Exploded View

1. To generate the exploded view, click **Drawing Views > Base View** on the Toolbar; the **Drawing View** dialog appears.
2. On the **Drawing View** dialog, select **Representation > Storyboard2**.
3. Select **Orientation > HOME**.
4. Set **Style** to **Visible Edges**.
5. Set **Scale** to **1:2**.
6. Set **Tangent Edges** to **Full Length** ⬚ .
7. Place the view at the center of the drawing sheet.
8. Click **OK**.

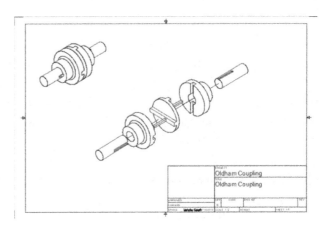

## Creating the Parts list

1. To create a parts list, click **Tables > Table** on the Toolbar; the **Table** dialog appears.

2. Select the exploded view from the drawing sheet.
3. Place the part list above the title block.

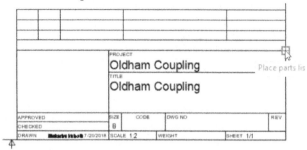

The balloons are added to the view, automatically.

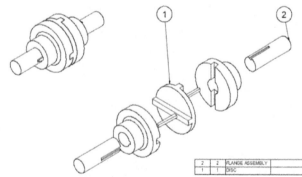

Notice that the components of the sub-assembly are not displayed in the parts list. Also, the balloons are not added to the components of the sub-assembly.

## Creating the Parts list of the sub-assembly

To create the parts list of the sub-assembly, you need to create a new drawing.

1. Open the Oldham Coupling assembly file.
2. On the Application Bar, click **File > New Drawing > From Design**.
3. Uncheck the **Full Assembly** option on the **Create Drawing** dialog.
4. Select the Flange Assembly from the Browser.

5. On the **Create Drawing** dialog, select **Drawing > Untitled**.
6. Select **Sheet > Create New Sheet**.
7. Click **OK**.
8. On the **Drawing View** dialog, select **Orientation > HOME**.
9. Select **Scale > 1:1**.
10. Select **Tangent Edges > Full Length**.
11. Place the drawing view at the location, as shown.
12. Click **OK**.

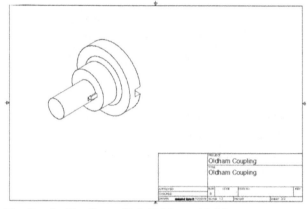

13. On the Toolbar, click Tables > Table.

    The view is selected, automatically.

14. Place the parts list table above the title block.

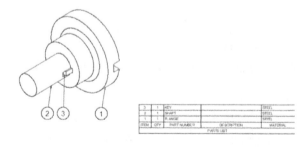

15. Double-click in the title block and change the title to Flange Assembly.
16. Click **OK**.
17. Right click on the Sheet2 at the bottom left corner.
18. Select **Rename Sheet**.

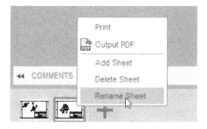

19. Type **Flange Assembly** and press Enter.

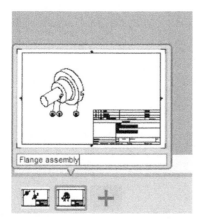

## Saving the Drawing

1. Click **Save** on the **Application Bar**.
2. Type-in **Oldham_Coupling Drawing** in the **Name** box.
3. Click **Save** to save the file.
4. Close the Oldham Coupling assembly and Oldham Coupling Drawing files.

# Chapter 5: Sketching

In this chapter, you will learn the sketching tools. You will learn to create:

- Rectangles
- Polygons
- Resolve Sketch
- Constraints
- Splines
- Ellipses
- Circles
- Arcs
- Circular pattern
- Trim Entities
- Fillets and Chamfers

## Creating Rectangles

A rectangle is a four sided object. You can create a rectangle by just specifying its two diagonal corners. However, there are various tools to create a rectangle. You can access these tools from the **Rectangle** menu available on the **Sketch** panel of the Toolbar. These tools are explained next.

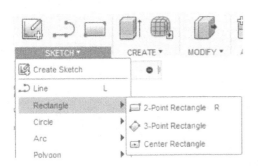

1. On the Toolbar, click **Sketch > Create Sketch** and select the XY plane.
2. On the Toolbar, click **Sketch > Rectangle menu > 2-Point Rectangle** .
3. Select the origin point to define the first corner.
4. Move the pointer diagonally and click to define the second corner.

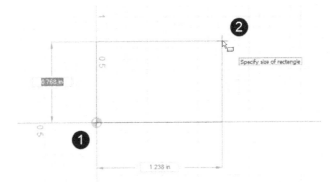

5. On the Toolbar, click **Sketch > Rectangle menu > Center Rectangle**.

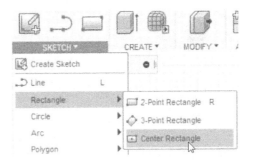

6. Click in the graphics window to define the center point.
7. Move the pointer and click to define the corner.

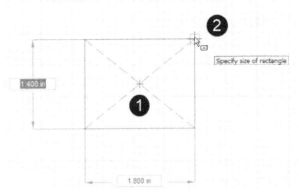

8. On the Toolbar, click **Sketch > Rectangle menu > 3-Point Rectangle**. This option creates a slanted rectangle.
9. Select two points to define the width and inclination angle of the rectangle.

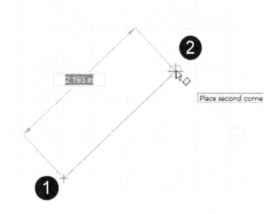

10. Select the third point to define its height.

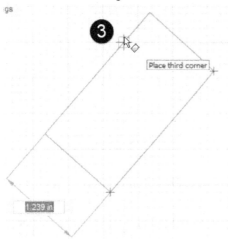

# Creating Polygons

A Polygon is a shape having many sides ranging from 3 to 1024. In Fusion 360, you can create regular polygons having sides with equal length. You can create a polygon using three methods. These methods are discussed next.

## Circumscribed Polygon

The circumscribed polygon has its sides touching an imaginary circle.

1. Start a sketch.
2. On the Toolbar, click **Sketch > Polygon > Circumscribed Polygon**.
3. Specify the center point of the polygon.
4. Type **8** in the **Edge Number** box displayed on the polygon.
5. Move the pointer and click to define the size and orientation of the polygon.

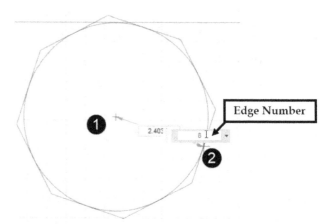

## Inscribed Polygon

The inscribed polygon has its vertices touching an imaginary circle.

1. On the Toolbar, click **Sketch > Polygon > Inscribed Polygon** .
2. Click to define the center of the polygon.
3. Type 6 in the Edges Number box.
4. Move the pointer and click to define the size and angle of the polygon.

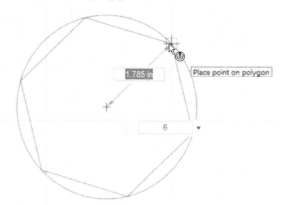

## Edge Polygon

In this method, you will create a polygon by specifying the length of one side, and then specifying the number of sides.

1. On the Toolbar, click **Sketch > Polygon > Edge Polygon**.
2. Specify the start point of one side.
3. Move the pointer and click to specify the length and angle of the side.

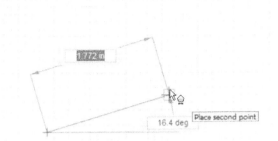

4. Type-in a value in the **Edge number** box.
5. Click to specify the side of the polygon.

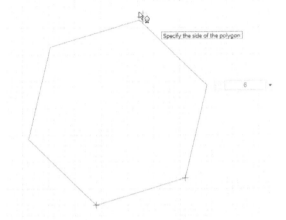

# Constraints

Constraints are used to control the shape of a sketch by establishing relationships between the sketch elements. You can add constraints using the tools available in the **Constraints** section of the **Sketch Palette**.

## Coincident

This constrain connects a point to another point.

1. On the **Sketch Palette**, click **Constraints > Coincident** .
2. Select two points. The selected points are connected together.

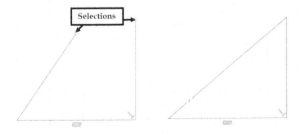

## Collinear

This constrain makes two lines collinear to each other.

1. On the **Sketch Palette**, click **Constraints > Collinear** .
2. Select the two lines in the sequence, as shown.

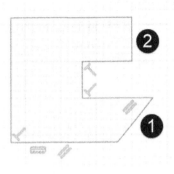

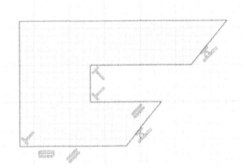

## Horizontal/Vertical Constraint

This option is used to apply the Horizontal or Vertical constraint. To apply the **Horizontal Constraint**, click on a line which is more inclined to the horizontal axis of the sketch. Next, click the **Horizontal/Vertical** icon on the **Sketch Palette**.

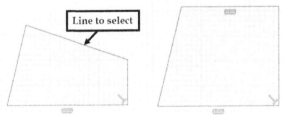

You can also align two points or vertices horizontally. Click the **Horizontal/Vertical** icon, and then select the two points.

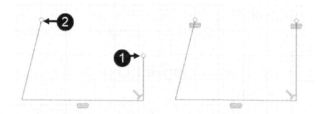

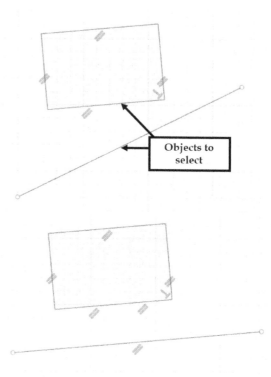

Use the **Horizontal/Vertical** option to apply the vertical constraint to a line that is inclined to the vertical axis. You can also use this option to align two points or vertices vertically.

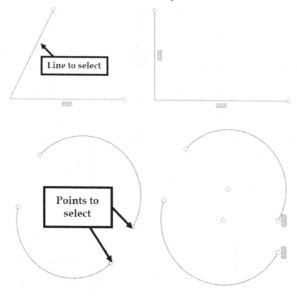

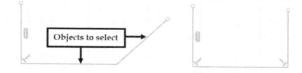

## ⚲ Perpendicular

Use the **Perpendicular** constraint to make two entities perpendicular to each other.

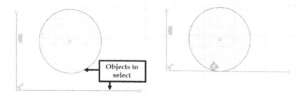

## ⟲ Tangent

This constraint makes an arc, circle, or line tangent to another arc or circle. Click the **Tangent** icon in the **Constraints** section of the Sketch Palette. Select a circle, arc, or line. Next, select another circle, or arc; the two elements will be tangent to each other.

## △ Midpoint

Use the **Midpoint** constraint to make a point coincide with the midpoint of a line or arc.

1. Press the Ctrl key and select a line/arc and a point.
2. Click the **Midpoint** icon on the Sketch Palette.

## ⫽ Parallel

Use the **Parallel** constraint to make two lines parallel to each other. To do this, click the **Parallel** icon in the **Constraints** section of the Sketch Palette. Next, select the two lines to be parallel to each other.

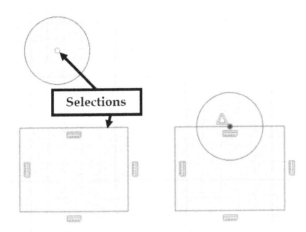

## ⊏⊐ Symmetry

Use the **Symmetry** constraint to make two sides of a sketch symmetrical about a line.

1. Create a sketch, as shown.

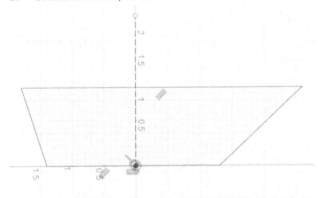

2. On the Sketch Palette, click **Constraints > Symmetry**.
3. Select the two inclined lines.
4. Select the construction line displayed at the center to define the symmetric line.

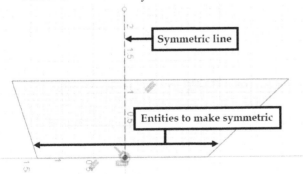

The symmetry constraint is applied between the two entities.

## Automatic Constraints

Fusion 360 automatically adds constraints when you create sketch elements.

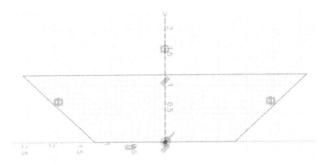

1. Start a new sketch and activate the **Line** tool from the **Sketch** panel of the Toolbar.
2. Click to specify the start point of the line.
3. Move the pointer in the horizontal direction and notice the **Horizontal** constraint flag.
4. Click to create a line with the **Horizontal** constraint.

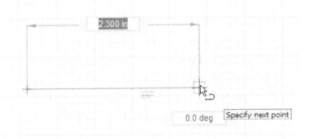

5. Move the pointer vertically in the upward direction and notice the **Perpendicular** constraint flag.
6. Click to create a line with the **Perpendicular** constraint.

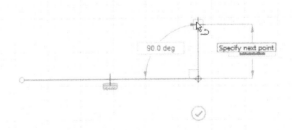

7. Create an inclined line as shown.

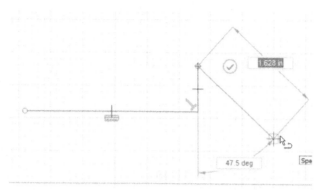

8. Move the pointer along the inclined line and notice the **Parallel** constraint flag.

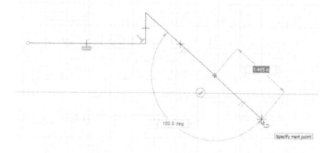

## Deleting Constraints

You can delete constraints by using the following method.

- On the Sketch Palette, check the **Show Constraints** option. You can uncheck this option to hide the constraints.
- Select the constraint and press **Delete** on your keyboard.

9. On the Toolbar, click **Sketch** panel > **Circle** > **Center Diameter Circle**, and then create circle.
10. Activate the **Line** tool and click on the circle.
11. Move the pointer around the circle and notice that the line maintains the **Tangent** constraint with the circle at a particular position.

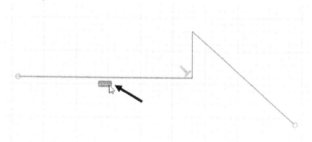

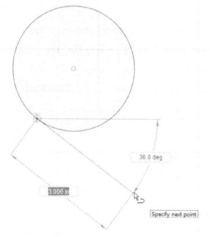

## Project

The **Project** tool helps you to use the edges of the part geometry to create sketch elements.

1. Download the Chapter 5: Sketching folder by reaching us at online.books999@gmail.com.
2. Open the Project_geometry part file from the folder.
3. Start a sketch on the plane offset to the model face, as shown.

12. Click to create a line that is tangent and coincident to the circle. Right click and select **OK**.

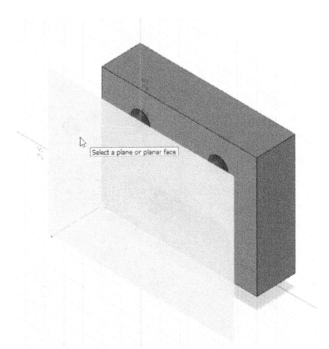

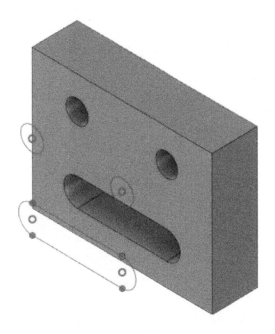

4. On the Toolbar, click **Sketch >**

   **Project/Include > Project** .
5. Click on the edges of the model, as shown.

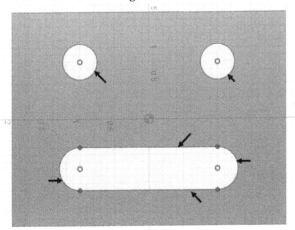

6. Click **OK**.
7. Click **Stop Sketch** on the **Sketch Palette**.

The selected edges are projected onto the sketch plane. Also, they are displayed in the magenta color.

## Conic Curve

The **Conic Curve** tool is used to create a conic curve. You can use a conic curve to connect two open sketch entities.

1. Create a triangle using the **Polygon** tool.
2. On the Toolbar, click **Sketch > Conic Curve**.
3. Select the start and end limits, and control point, as shown.

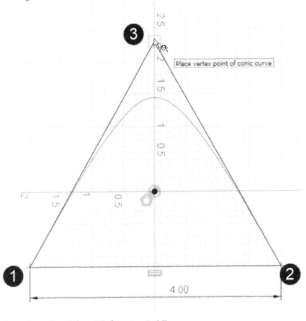

4. Set the **Rho** Value to **0.25**.

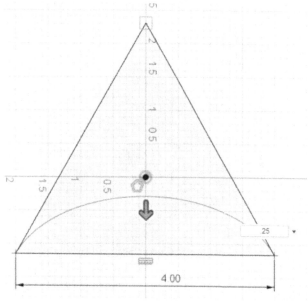

5. Set the **Rho** Value to **0.75** and press Enter.

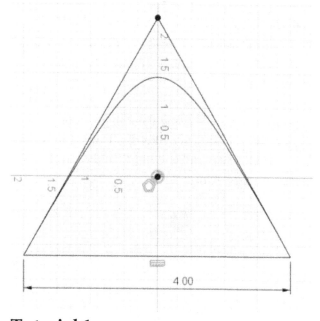

# Tutorial 1

In this tutorial, you will create a sketch using the **Line**, **3-Point Arc**, and **Circle** tools.

1. Activate the **Sketch** Environment.

2. On the Toolbar, click **Sketch > Line** .

3. Click on the origin point to define the start point of the line.

4. Move the pointer horizontally toward right and click.

5. Move the pointer upward and click.

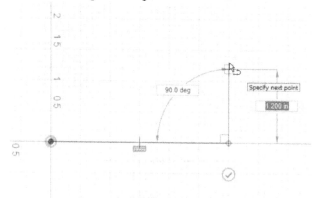

6. Right click and select **OK**.

7. On the Toolbar, click **Sketch > Arc** drop-down > **3-Point Arc**.

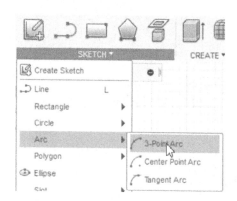

8. Specify the three points of the arc, as shown.

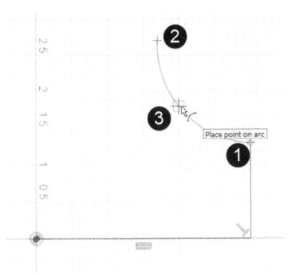

9. On the Sketch Palette, click **Options >**
   **Construction** ◁.
10. On the Toolbar, click **Sketch > Line**.
11. Select the origin point of the sketch, move the
    pointer vertically upwards, and click. Press Esc.

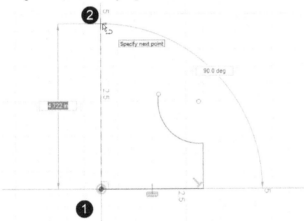

12. On the Toolbar, click **Sketch > Mirror.**

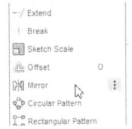

13. Select the arc, horizontal, and vertical lines.
14. On the **Mirror** dialog, click the **Mirror line**
    button and select the vertical construction line.
    Click **OK**.

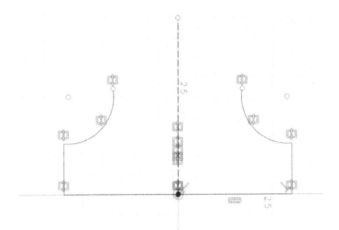

15. On the Sketch Palette, click **Options >**
    **Construction** ◁.
16. On the Toolbar, click **Sketch > Arc drop-down >**
    **3-Point Arc**.
17. Select the end points of the left and right arcs,
    and then move the pointer upward and click.

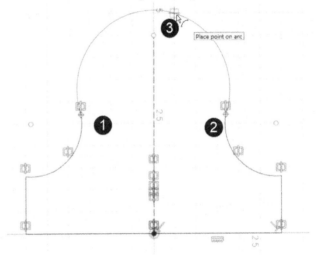

18. Right click and select **OK**.
19. On the Toolbar, click **Sketch > Circle** drop-
    down > **Center Diameter Circle**.
20. Select the centerpoint of the three-point arc,
    move the pointer outward, and click to create
    the circle.

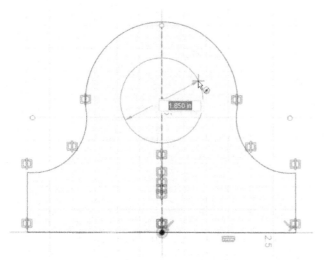

21. On the Sketch Palette, click **Constraints >**
    **Tangent** ⌀.
22. Select two arcs, as shown.

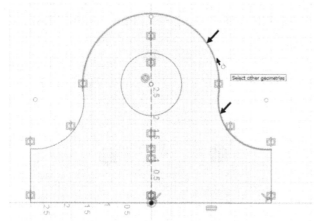

23. Add dimensions to the sketch, as shown.

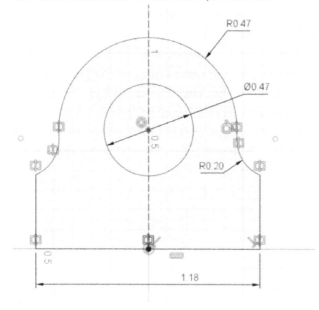

24. On the Sketch Palette, click **Constraints >**
    **Coincident**.
25. Select the centerpoint of the arc and the vertical
    line, as shown.

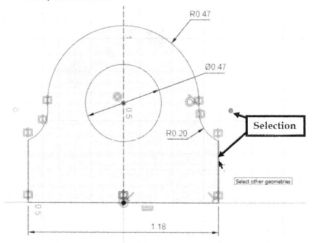

26. Add the dimension between the circle and the
    horizontal line, as shown.

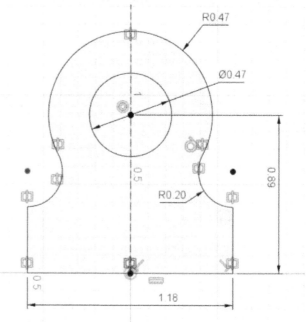

27. Click **Stop Sketch** on the Toolbar.

## Ellipses

Ellipses are also non-uniform curves, but they have
a regular shape. They are actually splines created in
regular closed shapes.

1. Activate the **Sketch** environment.

2. On the Toolbar, click **Sketch > Ellipse**  .
3. Pick a point in the graphics window to define the center of the ellipse.
4. Move the pointer and click to define the radius and orientation of the first axis.

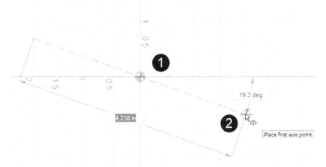

5. Move the pointer and click to define the radius of the second axis.

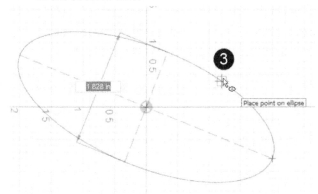

Click and drag the ellipse the notice that it is under-defined. You need to add dimensions and constrains to fully define the ellipse.

6. On the Sketch Palette, click **Options > Construction** .
7. Activate the **Line** tool and select the centerpoint of the ellipse.
8. Move the pointer horizontally toward right and click. Press Esc.

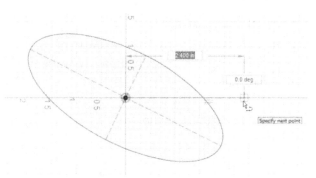

9. On the Toolbar, click **Sketch > Sketch Dimension**.
10. Select the horizontal line and the major axis of the ellipse.
11. Move the pointer between the selected lines and click to position the angled dimension.

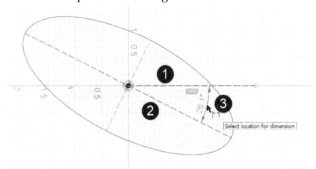

12. Type 15 and press Enter.
13. Select the major axis.
14. Move the pointer downward and click to position the dimension.
15. Type 1.96 and press Enter.
16. Likewise, add the dimension to the minor axis. This fully-defines the sketch.

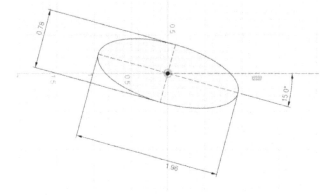

## Concentric Constraint

Use the **Concentric** Constraint to make two centerpoints of circles, arcs, or ellipses coincident with each other.

1. Create two circles, as shown.

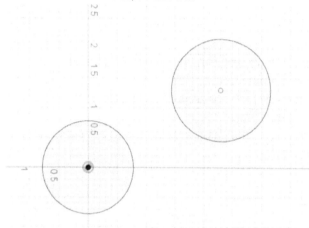

2. On the Sketch Palette, click **Constraint >**

   **Concentric** ⊚ .
3. Select the two circles to make them concentric.

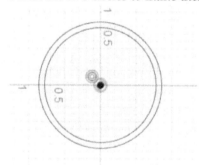

4. Press Esc.
5. On the Toolbar, click **Sketch > Sketch**

   **Dimension** ⊢⊣ .
6. Select the inner circle, move the point upward, and click to position the dimension.
7. Type 1.96 and press Enter.
8. Likewise, add dimension to the remaining circle and change its value to 5.5.
9. Press Esc.

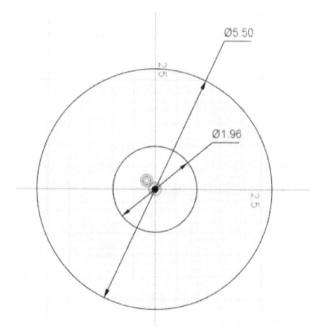

## Center Point Arc

The Center Point Arc tool creates an arc by using three points (center, start, and end points).

1. On the Toolbar, click **Sketch > Arc** drop-down **>**

   **Center Point Arc** ⌒ .
2. Select the point on the circle as shown below.

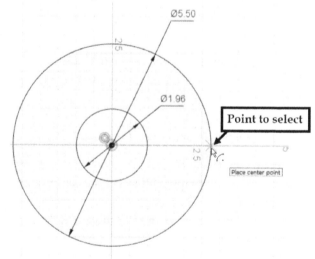

3. Move the pointer down and click on the circle.

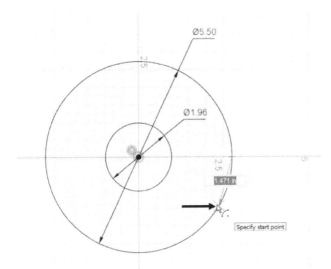

4. Move the pointer leftwards and up, and then click on the circle.

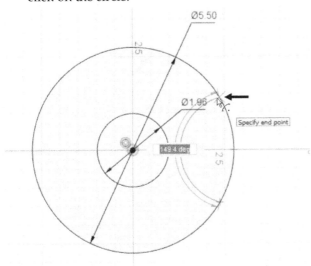

5. Right click and select **OK**.
6. On the Toolbar, click **Sketch > Sketch Dimension** .
7. Select the arc, move the pointer, and then click to position the dimension.
8. Type 0.98, and then press Enter.

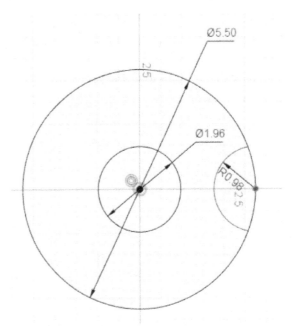

9. On the Sketch Palette, click **Constraints > Horizontal/Vertical** .
10. Click on the centerpoints of the circle and arc.

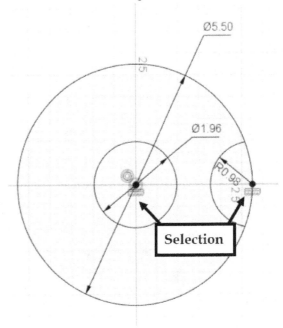

## Circular Pattern

The **Circular Pattern** tool creates an arrangement of objects around a point in circular form.

1. On the Toolbar, click **Sketch > Circular Pattern**  .

2. Select the arc.
3. Click the Select button next to the **Center Point** option.
4. Select the center of the circle; the preview of the circular pattern appears.

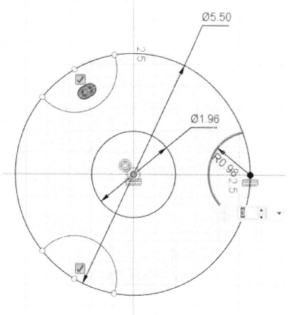

5. Type **4** in the **Quantity** box.
6. Select **Type > Full**.
7. Click **OK**.

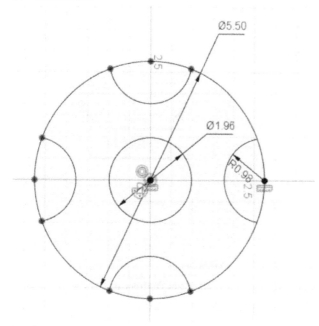

# Trim

The **Trim** tool removes the unwanted entities of a sketch using a trimming element.

1. On the Toolbar, click **Sketch > Trim** .
2. Click on the portions of the sketch, as shown.

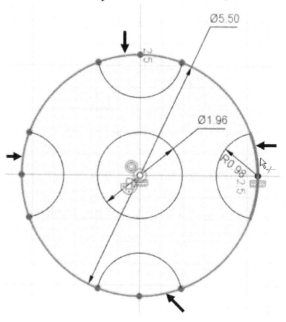

3. Right click and select **OK**.

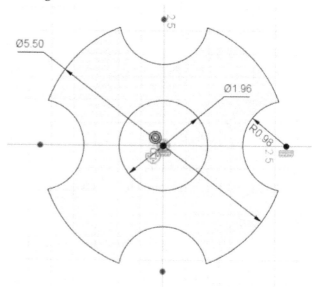

4. Click **Stop Sketch**.

# Extend

The **Extend** tool is similar to the **Trim** tool but its use is opposite of it. This tool is used to extend lines, arcs and other open entities to connect to other objects.

1. Create a sketch as shown below.

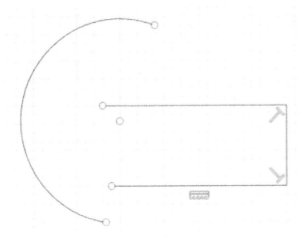

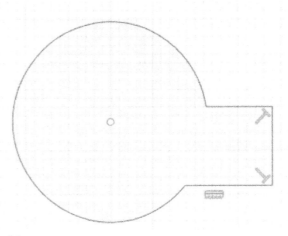

2.   Click **Sketch > Extend** on the Toolbar.
3.   Select the horizontal open line. This will extend the line up to the arc.

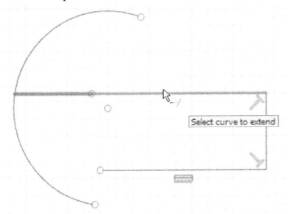

Likewise, extend the other elements, as shown.

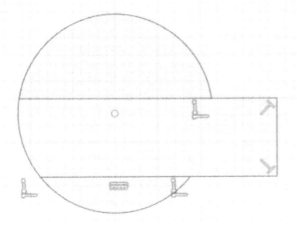

4.   Trim the unwanted portions.

## Offset

The **Offset** tool creates parallel copies of lines, circles, arcs and so on.

1.   On the Toolbar, click **Sketch > Offset**.
2.   Select an entity and notice that all the connected entities are selected.
3.   Type-in the offset distance in the value box attached to the offset copy.
4.   Click **Flip** icon to define the offset side.

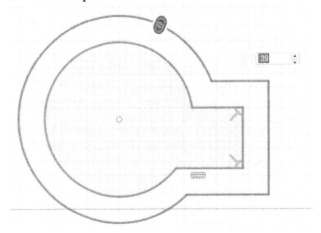

5.   Click **OK**.

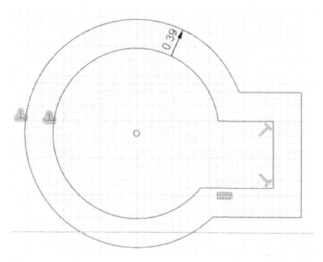

## Text

Texts are used to provide information on the models such as company name, model specifications, and so on.

1.  Start a new sketch.

2.  On the Toolbar, click **Sketch** panel > **Text** **A** .
3.  Specify a point in the graphics window.
4.  Click in the **Text** box in the **Text** dialog, and then type FUSION 360.
5.  On the **Text** dialog, set Text Style to Bold.
6.  Select **Font > Arial**.
7.  On the dialog, use the **Horizontal Flip** or **Vertical Flip** icons to flip the text.
8.  Type 0.45 in the **Height** box.
9.  Click and drag the angle handle displayed in the graphics window (or) type-in a value in the **Angle** box.

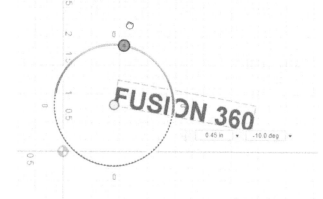

10. Click **OK**.

# Chapter 6: Additional Modeling Tools

In this chapter, you create models using additional modeling tools. You will learn to:

- Create slots
- Create circular patterns
- Create holes
- Create chamfers
- Create shells
- Create rib features
- Create coils
- Create a loft feature
- Create a thread
- Create a sweep feature
- Replace faces
- Create a variable fillet

## TUTORIAL 1

In this tutorial, you create the model shown in figure:

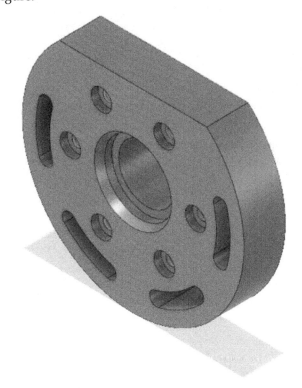

### Creating the First Feature

1. Create a new project with the name **Autodesk Fusion 360 Basics Tutorial** (See Chapter 2, Tutorial 1, Creating New Project section to learn how to create a new project).
2. Click the **Create sketch** button on the **Sketch** panel of the Toolbar, and select the XY Plane.

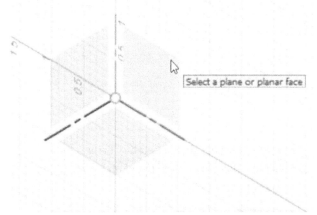

3. Click **Sketch > Circle > Center Diameter Circle** on the Toolbar.
4. Draw a circle by selecting the origin point as it center (See Chapter 2, Tutorial 1, Starting a Sketch section to learn how to create a new circle).
5. Click the **Line** button.
6. Specify a point at top left outside the circle.
7. Move the pointer horizontally and notice the Horizontal constraint symbol.
8. Click outside the circle. Press Esc to deactivate the **Line** tool.

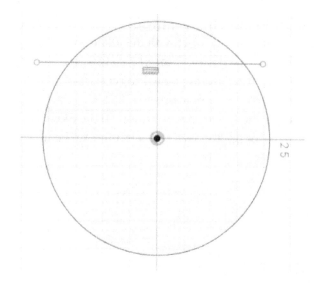

9. On the Toolbar, click **Sketch > Trim** ⌐.
10. Click on the portions of the sketch to trim, as shown below.

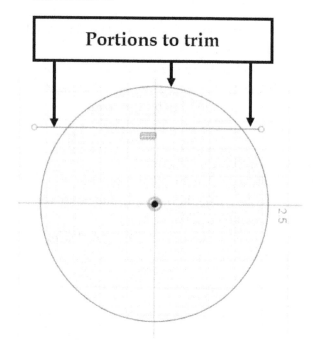

11. Activate the **Sketch Dimension** tool and select the horizontal line.
12. Right click and select **Pick Circle/Arc Tangent**.
13. Select the bottom quadrant point of the arc.
14. Move the pointer toward left and click to place the dimension.
15. Type 1.102 and press Enter.
16. Select the arc and place the dimension.

17. Type 0.63 and press Enter.

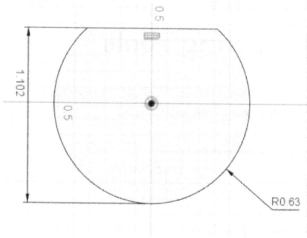

18. Click **Sketch > Slot drop-down > Center Two Point Arc Slot** on the Toolbar.

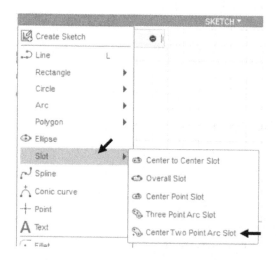

19. Select the origin as the center point.
20. Move the cursor outward and click in the first quadrant of the circle to specify the start point of the slot arc.
21. Move the cursor and click in the fourth quadrant of the circle to specify the end point of the slot arc.

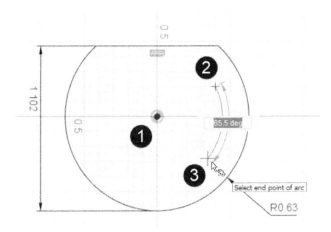

22. Move the cursor outward from the arc and click.

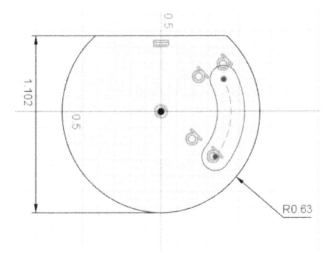

23. Click Sketch > Sketch **Dimension** button on Toolbar.
24. Select the start point of the slot arc.
25. Select the center point of the slot arc.
26. Select the end point of the slot arc.

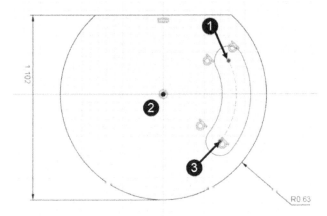

27. Place the angular dimension of the slot.
28. Enter **30** in the box and press Enter.

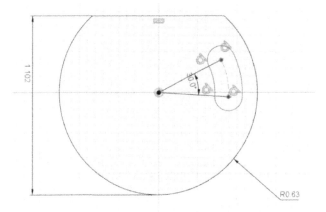

29. Click the **Construction** button on the **Sketch Palette**.

30. Click the **Line** button on the **Sketch** panel.
31. Draw a horizontal line passing through the origin.

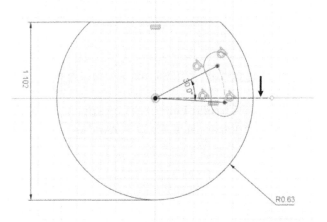

32. Click the **Symmetry** button on the **Sketch Palette**.
33. Select the end caps of the slot.
34. Select the construction line; the slot is made symmetric about the construction line.

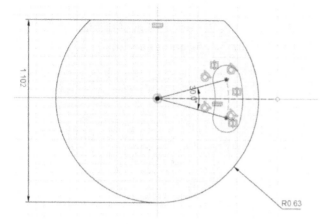

35. Apply the other dimensions to the slot.

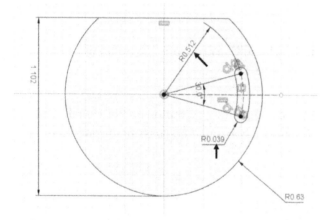

36. On the Toolbar, click **Sketch > Circular Pattern** ; the **Circular Pattern** dialog appears.

37. On the Toolbar, click **Select > Window Selection**.

38. Select all the elements of the slot by creating a selection window(press and hold the left mouse button and drag the pointer from left to right).

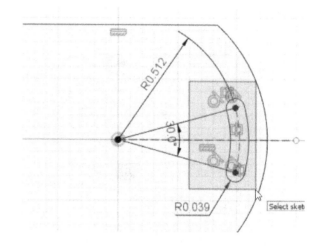

39. Click the **Select** button located on the right-side of the **Center Point** option.
40. Select the origin point of the sketch.
41. Enter **4** in the **Quantity** box.
42. Select **Type > Angle**.
43. Type **-180** in the **Total Angle** box.

The preview of the circular pattern appears.

44. Click **OK** to create the circular pattern.

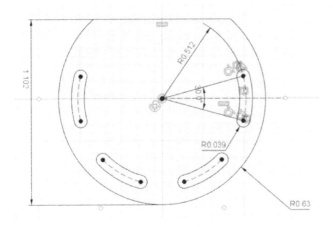

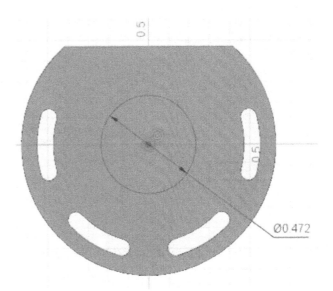

45. Click the **Stop Sketch** button on the Toolbar.
46. Extrude the sketch up to 0.236 distance (See Chapter 2, Tutorial 1, Creating the Base Feature section to learn how to create an extruded feature).

2. Extrude the sketch up to 0.078 distance.

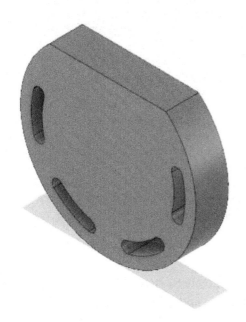

## Adding the Second feature

1. Create a sketch on the back face of the model (use the Orbit ⊕ tool available on the Navigation bar to rotate the model).

## Creating a Counterbore Hole

In this section, you will create a counterbore hole concentric to the cylindrical face.

1. On the Toolbar, click **Create > Hole**; the **Hole** dialog appears.
2. Set the parameters in the **Hole** dialog, as shown in figure.

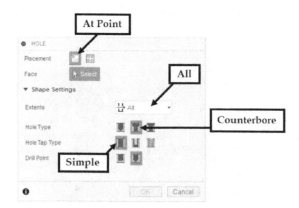

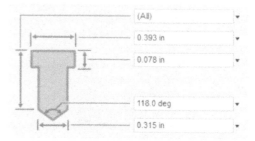

3. Click on the front face of the model; the preview of the hole appears.

Now, you need to specify the reference.

4. Select the circular edge of the front face; the hole is made concentric to the edge.

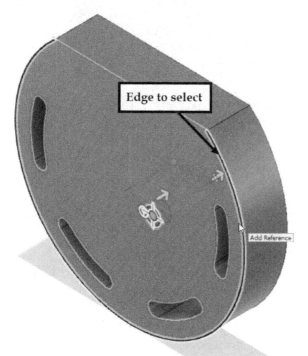

5. Specify the size values on the **Hole** dialog, as shown.

6. Click **OK**; the counterbore hole is created.

## Creating a Threaded hole
In this section, you will create a hole using a sketch point.

1. Click the **Create Sketch** button on the Sketch panel and select the front face of the model.

2. On the Toolbar, click **Sketch > Point**.

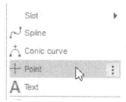

3. Place the point on the front face of the model.

4. Click the **Horizontal /Vertical** button on the Sketch Palette.

5. Select the point and sketch origin; the point becomes horizontal to the origin.

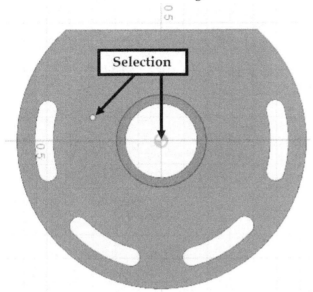

6. Create a horizontal dimension of 0.354 between the point and origin.

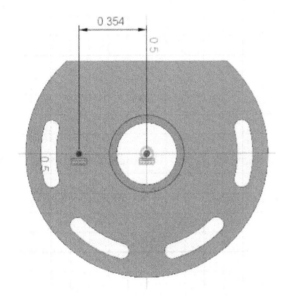

7. Click **Stop Sketch**.
8. On the Toolbar, click **Create > Hole**; the **Hole** dialog appears.
9. Select the sketch point.
10. Select **Extents > All**.
11. Select the **Counterbore** ![icon] option.
12. Select the **Tapped** ![icon] option.
13. Set **Thread Offset** to **Full** ![icon].

14. Set the **Counterbore Diameter** to 0.118.
15. Set the **Counterbore Depth** to 0.039.
16. Set the **Thread Type** to **ANSI Unified Screw Threads**.
17. Set the **Size** to **0.073**.
18. Set the **Designation** to **1-64 UNC**.
19. Select **Class > 2B**.
20. Set the **Direction** to **Right Hand**.

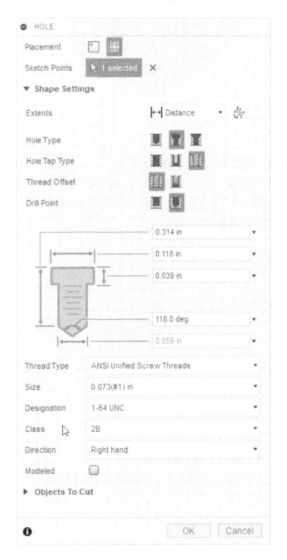

21. Click **OK** to create the hole.

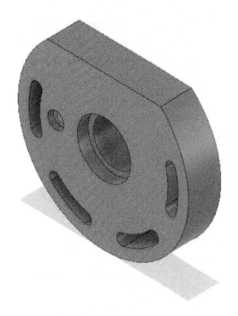

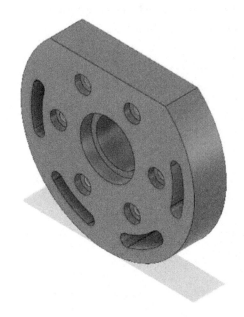

## Creating a Circular Pattern

1. On the Toolbar, click **Create** panel > **Pattern** drop-down > **Circular Pattern**; the **Circular Pattern** dialog appears.

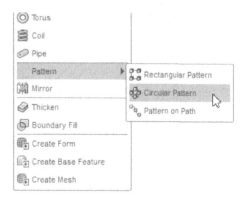

2. Select **Pattern Type > Features**.
3. Select the threaded hole created in the previous section.

4. Click the **Select** button next to the **Axis** option.
5. Select the outer cylindrical face of the model.
6. Select **Type > Full**.
7. Enter **6** in the **Quantity** box.
8. Click **OK** to create the circular pattern.

## Creating Chamfers

1. On the Toolbar, click **Modify > Chamfer**.

2. Select **Chamfer Type > Distance and angle** on the dialog.
3. Select the circular edge of the counterbore hole.

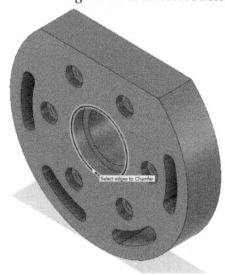

4. Enter 0.022 in the **Distance** box and 60 in the **Angle** box.

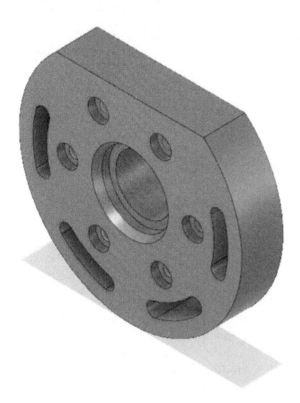

5. Click **OK** to create the chamfer.

## Saving the Part

1. Click **Save** 💾 on the **Application bar**.
2. On the **Save** window, type-in Ch6_tut1 in the **Name** box.
3. Click the down arrow button next to the **Location** box.
4. Select **Autodesk Fusion 360 Basics Tutorial** from the **Project** list.
5. Click **Save** to save the file.
6. Click the **Close** icon on the file tab.

# TUTORIAL 2

In this tutorial, you will create the model shown in figure.

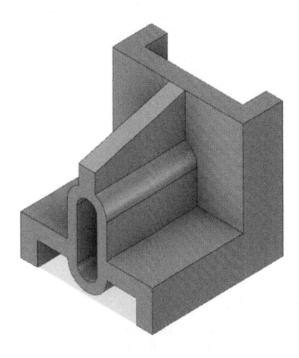

## Creating the first feature

1. On the Toolbar, click **Sketch > Create Sketch**
   .

2. Select the YZ plane.

3. Draw an L-shaped sketch using the **Line** tool and dimension it.

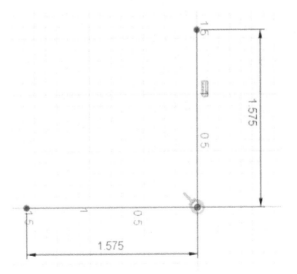

4. On the Toolbar, click **Sketch > Offset** .
5. Select the sketch, and then drag the offset handle in the upward direction.

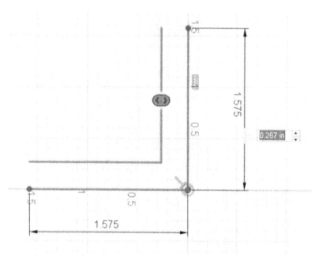

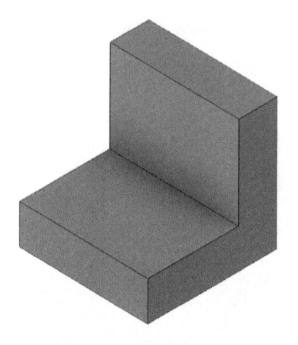

6. Type 0.472 in the **Offset position** box.
7. Click **OK**.
8. Click the **Line** button and draw lines closing the offset sketch.

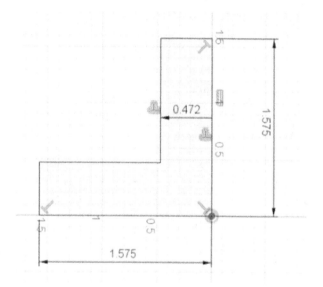

## Creating the Shell feature

You can create a shell feature by removing a face of the model and applying thickness to other faces.

1. Click **Modify > Shell** on the Toolbar; the **Shell** dialog appears.

Now, you need to select the faces to remove.

9. Click **Stop Sketch**.

10. Click **Create > Extrude** on the Toolbar.
11. Click in the region enclosed by the sketch.
12. Select **Direction > Symmetric** option from the **Extrude** dialog.
13. Set **Measurement** to **Whole Length** .
14. Set the **Distance** to 1.575.
15. Click **OK** to create the first feature.
16. Click the **Home** icon next to the ViewCube.

2. Select the top face and the back face of the model.

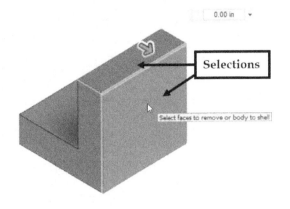

3.  Select the front face and the bottom face of the model.

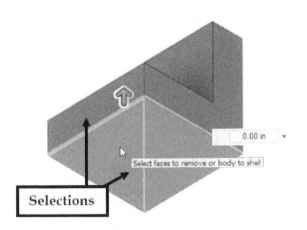

4.  Set **Thickness** to 0.197.
5.  Click **OK** to shell the model.

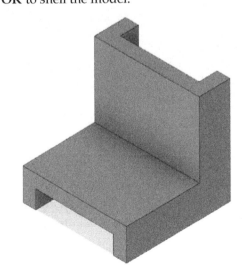

## Creating the Third feature

1.  Click **Sketch > Create Sketch** on the Toolbar.

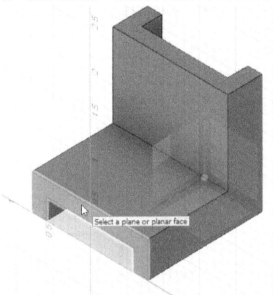

2.  Select the front face of the model.
3.  Click **Sketch > Slot** drop-down **> Center to Center Slot** on the Toolbar.

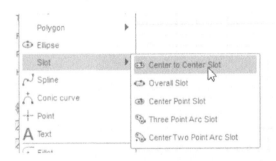

4.  Draw a slot by selecting the first, second, and third points, as shown.

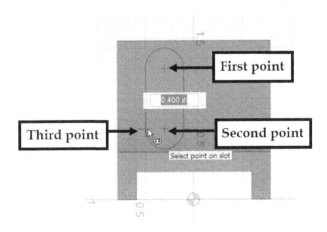

5.  On the Sketch Palette, click **Constraints >**

**Midpoint**.

6. Select the lower center point of the slot.
7. Select the lower horizontal edge of the model, as shown.

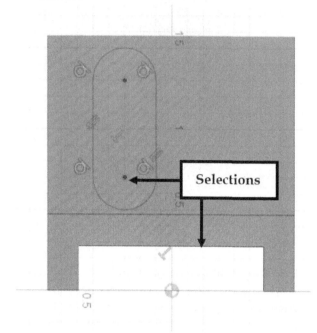

8. Apply dimensions to the slot.

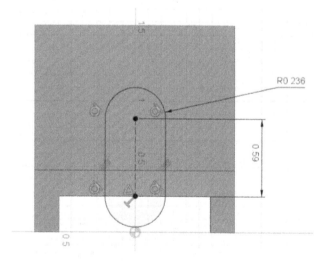

9. Click **Stop Sketch**.
10. Click **Create > Extrude** on the Toolbar.
11. Click in the three regions of the sketch.

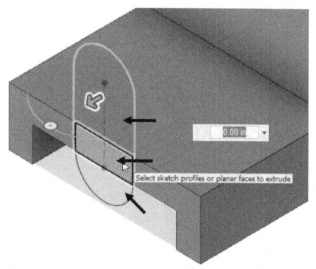

12. Select the **To Object** option from the **Extent** drop-down.
13. Press and hold the left mouse button on the top face, and then select the back face from the dialog.

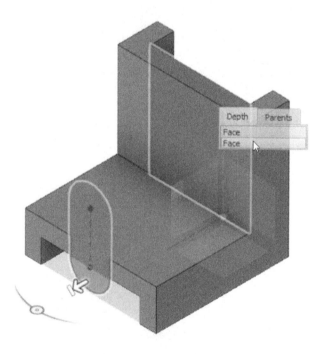

14. Select **Chain Faces > Extend Faces** .
15. Select **Operation > Join** from the dialog.
16. Click **OK** to create the feature.

88

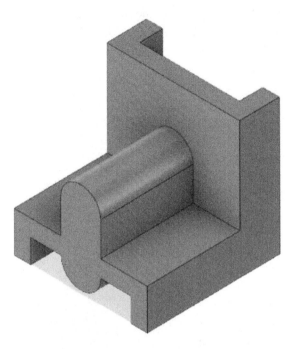

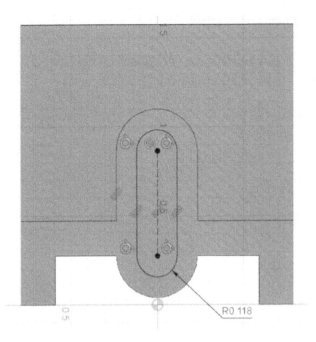

## Creating a Cut Feature

1. Start a sketch on the front face of the model.
2. Click **Sketch > Slot** drop-down > **Center to Center Slot**.
3. Create a vertical slot.
4. On the Sketch Palette, click **Constraints > Concentric**.
5. Select a slot end cap.
6. Select a circular edge of the model; the slot end cap is made concentric with the circular edge.
7. Likewise, make the other end cap of the slot concentric to circular edge.
8. Add a dimension to the sketch, as shown.

9. Stop the sketch.
10. Click **Create > Extrude** on the Toolbar.
11. Click in the region enclosed by the sketch.
12. Select the **All** option from the **Extent** drop-down.
13. Select **Operation > Cut**.
14. Click the **Flip** icon, if the arrow on the sketch points in the forward direction.
15. Click **OK** to create the cut feature.

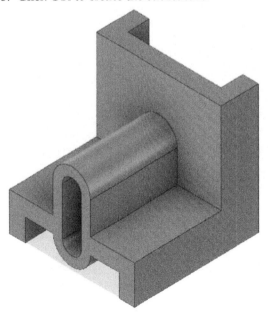

## Creating the Rib Feature

In this section, you will create a rib feature at the

middle of the model.

1. Click **Sketch > Create Sketch** on the Toolbar.
2. Expand the **Origin** folder, and then select the YZ Plane from the Browser.

3. Click **Sketch > Line** on the Toolbar.
4. Draw the sketch, as shown below.

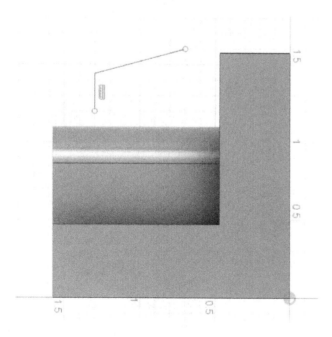

5. On the Sketch Palette, click **Constraints > Coincident**.

6. Select the end point of the inclined line and the vertex point of the top edge.

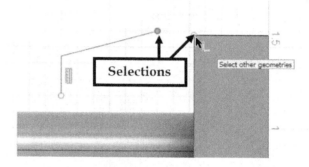

7. Select the end point of the vertical line and the vertical edge, as shown.

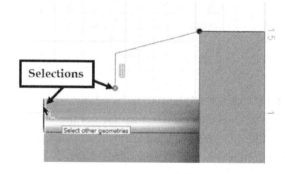

8. Select the endpoint of the vertical line and the vertical edge.

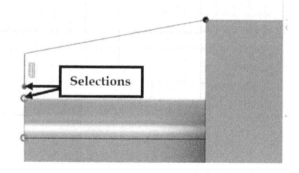

9. Add dimension to the sketch.

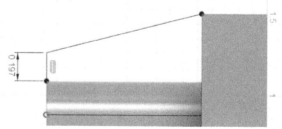

10. Stop the sketch.
11. Click **Create > Rib** on the Toolbar; the **Rib**

dialog appears.

12. Select the sketch.
13. Set **Thickness** to 0.197.
14. Select **Depth Options > To Next**.
15. Select **Thickness Options > Symmetric**.
16. Click **OK** to create the rib feature.

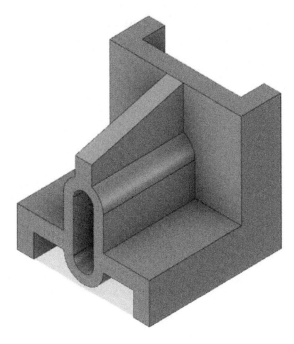

17. Save the model and close it.

# TUTORIAL 3

In this tutorial, you will create a helical spring using the **Coil** tool.

## Creating the Coil

1. Click **Create > Coil** on the Toolbar, and select the XZ Plane.

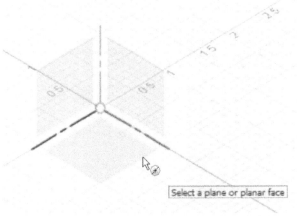

2. Select the origin point to define the center of the coil.
3. Move the cursor outward and click to create a circle.
4. On the **Coil** dialog, type **1.575** in the **Diameter** box.
5. Select **Type > Revolution and Pitch**.
6. Type **8** in the **Revolutions** box.
7. Type **0.59** in the **Pitch** box.
8. Select **Section > Circular**.
9. Select **Section Position > On Center**.
10. Type **0.236** in the **Section Size** box.

Click and drag the Angle handle and notice that the coil is tapered.

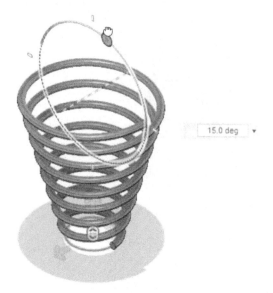

11. Type **0** in the **Angle** box.
12. Click **OK** to create the coil.
13. Save and close the file.

# TUTORIAL 4

In this tutorial, you create a shampoo bottle using the **Loft**, **Extrude**, **Press Pull**, and **Sweep** tools.

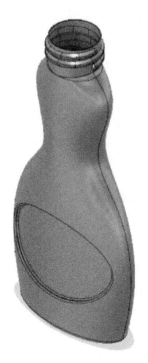

## Creating the First Section and Rails

To create a swept feature, you need to create sections and guide curves.

1. Click **Sketch > Create Sketch** on the Toolbar.
2. Select the XZ plane.

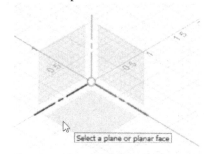

3. Click **Sketch > Ellipse** on the Toolbar.
4. Draw the ellipse by selecting the points, as shown.

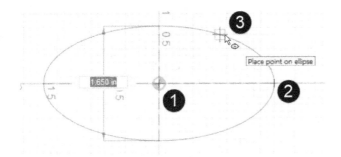

5. On the Toolbar, click **Sketch > Sketch Dimension**.
6. Select the ellipse, move the cursor downward, and click.
7. Type 1.968 and press Enter.
8. Select the ellipse, move the cursor toward left, and click.
9. Type 0.984 and press Enter.

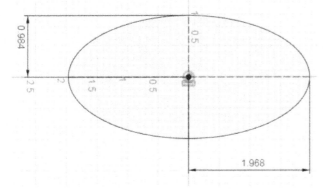

10. Click **Stop Sketch**.

11. Click **Sketch > Create Sketch** on the Toolbar.
12. Select the XY plane from the graphics window.

13. Click **Sketch > Spline > Fit Point Spline** on the Toolbar.
14. Select a point on the horizontal axis of the sketch; a rubber band curve is attached to the cursor

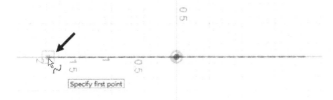

15. Move the cursor up and specify the second point

of the spline; a curve is attached to cursor.

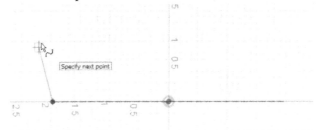

16. Move the cursor up and specify the third point.

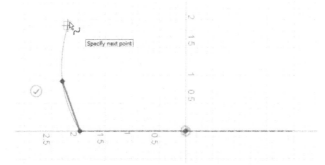

17. Likewise, specify the other points of the spline, as shown.
18. Click the right mouse button and select **OK**. The spline will be similar to the one shown in figure.

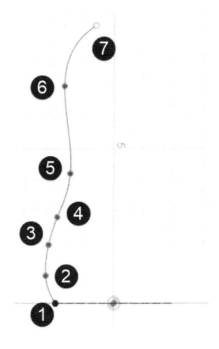

19. Right click and select **Sketch > Line** from the Marking Menu.
20. On the Sketch Palette, click **Options >**

Construction 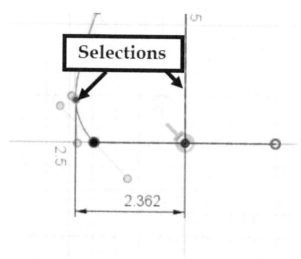.

21. Select the origin point of the sketch, move the pointer vertically upward and click to create a vertical construction line. Press Esc.

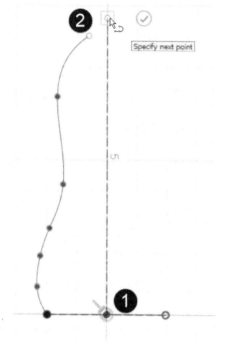

22. Make the first point of the spline coincident with the ellipse, if not already coincident.

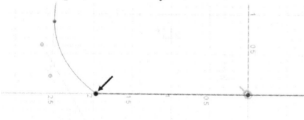

23. On the Toolbar, click **Sketch > Sketch Dimension**.
24. Select the second point of the spline and the construction line.
25. Move the cursor and click to place the dimension.
26. Type 2.362 in the box and press Enter.

27. Apply the other horizontal dimensions to the spline, as shown in figure.

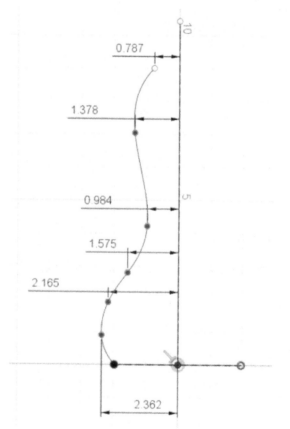

28. Select the origin point of the sketch and the top end point of the spline.
29. Move the pointer toward right and click.
30. Type 8.858 in the box and press Enter.

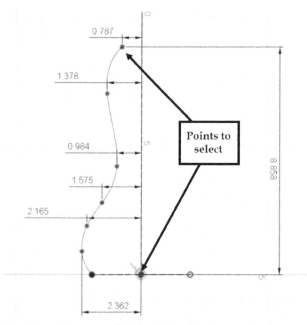

Points to select

31. Likewise, create other dimensions, as shown.

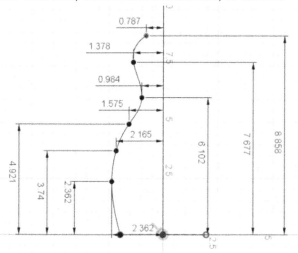

32. Click **Sketch > Mirror** 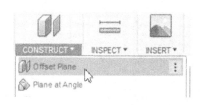 on the Toolbar; the **Mirror** dialog appears.
33. Select the spline. Make sure that you select the curve and not the points.
34. Click the **Select** button next to the **Mirror line** option on the **Mirror** dialog, and then select the construction line.
35. Click **OK**.

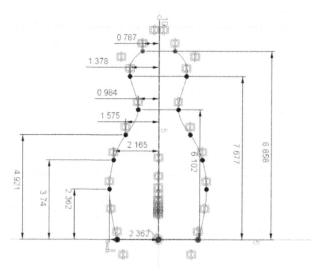

36. Click **Stop Sketch** on the **Toolbar**.

## Creating the second section

1. Click **Construct > Offset Plane** on the Toolbar.

2. Select the XZ plane from the Browser.

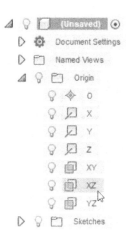

3. Enter **8.858** in the **Distance** box.

4. Click **OK**.
5. On the Toolbar, click **Sketch > Create Sketch**.
6. Select the newly created datum plane.
7. On the Toolbar, click **Sketch > Circle** drop-down > **2-Point Circle**.

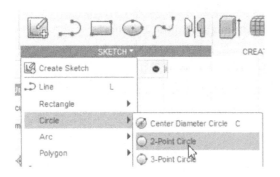

8. Select the end points of the two splines, as shown.

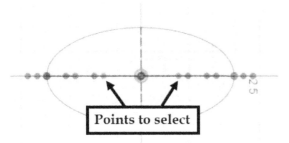

9. Right click and select **OK**.

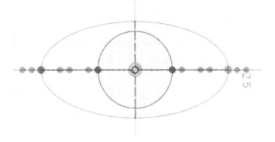

10. Click and drag the circle downward and notice that it is under-defined.

11. On the Sketch Palette, click **Constraints > Coincident** .
12. Select the centerpoint of the circle and the origin point of the sketch; the circle is fully-defined.
13. Click **Stop Sketch** on the Toolbar.

## Creating the Loft feature

1. To create a loft feature, click **Create > Loft** on the Toolbar; the **Loft** dialog appears.

2. Click in the region enclosed by the ellipse.
3. Click the plus $+$ icon in the **Profiles** section.
4. Click in the region enclosed by the circle.

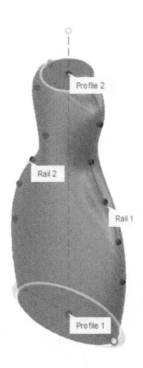

5. Select **Guide Type > Rails** option from the dialog.

6. Select the cursor icon next to the Rails option.
7. Select the first spline.
8. Click the plus ⁺ icon in the **Rails** section.
9. Select the second spline.

10. Click **OK** to create the loft feature.

## Creating the Extruded feature

1. Right click and select **Sketch > Create Sketch**.

2. Select the top face of the sweep feature.

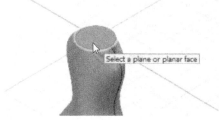

3. On the Toolbar, click **Sketch > Circle > Center Diameter Circle**.
4. Select the origin point, move the cursor outside, and click to create a circle.
5. Right click and select **OK**.
6. Right click and select **Sketch > Sketch Dimension**.
7. Select the circle, move the cursor outward, and click.
8. Type 1.574 and press Enter.

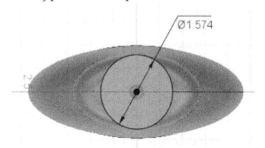

9. Click **Stop Sketch** on the Toolbar.
10. Click the **Extrude** button on the **Create** panel.
11. Extrude the circle up to 1 in.

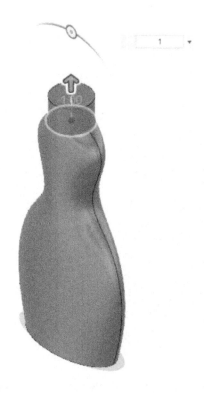

## Creating an Emboss

1. Click **Construct > Offset Plane** on the Toolbar.
2. Select the XY plane from the Browser.
3. Enter **2** in the **Distance** box and click **OK**.

4. Click **Sketch > Create Sketch** on the Toolbar.
5. Select the newly created datum plane
6. Click **Sketch > Ellipse** on the Toolbar.
7. Draw the ellipse by selecting the points, as shown.

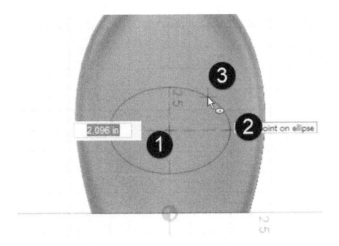

8. On the Toolbar, click **Sketch > Sketch Dimension**.
9. Select the ellipse, move the cursor downward, and click.
10. Type 2 and press Enter.
11. Select the ellipse, move the cursor toward left, and click.
12. Type 1.35 and press Enter.
13. Select the origin point of the sketch and the center point of the ellipse.
14. Move the cursor toward left and click to place the dimension between the selected point.
15. Type 2.55 and press Enter.
16. On the Sketch Palette, click **Constraints > Horizontal/Vertical**.
17. Select the center point of the ellipse and the sketch origin; the sketch is fully-constrained.
18. Click **Stop Sketch**.

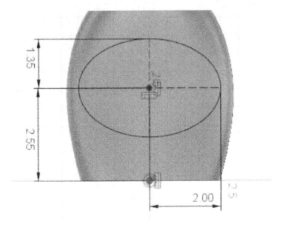

19. Click **Modify > Press Pull** on the Toolbar;

the **Press Pull** dialog appears.
20. Click in the region enclosed by the sketch.
21. Select **Extent > To Object**.
22. Click on the surface of the loft feature.
23. Set **Solution** to **Min Solution**.
24. Select **Chain Faces > Chain Faces**.
25. Set the **Offset** to -0.125.
26. Select **Operation > New Body**.
27. Click **OK** to create a new body.

28. On the Toolbar, click **Modify > Combine**.
29. Select the Target and Tool bodies, as shown.

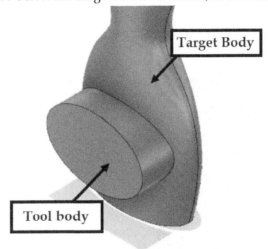

Target Body

Tool body

30. Select **Operation > Cut**.
31. Click **OK**.

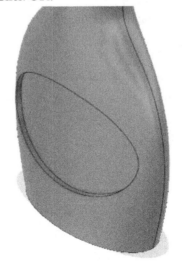

## Creating Fillets

1. Click **Modify > Fillet** on the Toolbar; the **Fillet** dialog appears.

2. Click on the bottom and top edges of the loft feature.

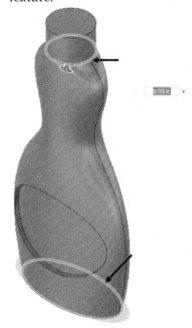

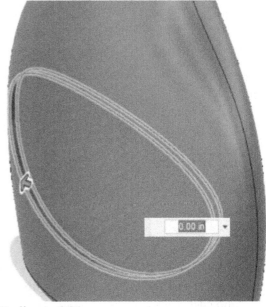

3. Select **Type > Constant Radius**.
4. Set **Radius** to 0.2.
5. Click **OK**.
6. Right click and select **Repeat Fillet**.

7. Select the edges of the emboss.

8. Set **Radius** to 0.04.
9. Click **OK**.

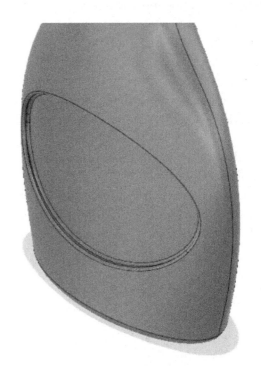

## Shelling the Model

1. Click **Modify > Shell** on the Toolbar; the **Shell** dialog appears.

2. Select the top face of the cylindrical feature.

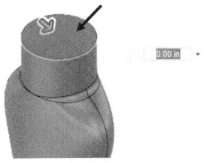

3. Set **Inside Thickness** to 0.03.
4. Click **OK** to create the shell.

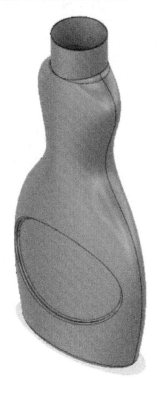

## Adding Threads

1. On the Toolbar, click **Construct > Offset Plane**.
2. Click on the top face of the model geometry.
3. Set the **Distance** value to -0.196.
4. Click **OK**; a new plane is created.

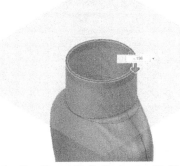

5. On the Toolbar, click **Create > Coil**.
6. Select the newly created plane.
7. Select the origin point of the sketch.
8. Click on the Top face of the ViewCube; the orientation is changed to top.
9. Select a point on the inner edge of the shell feature, as shown.

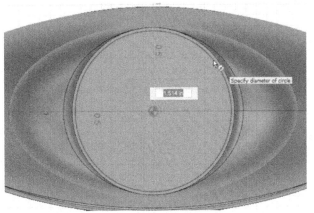

10. Click the **Home** icon located at the top left corner of the ViewCube; the view orientation is changed to Home.
11. Specify the settings on the **Coil** dialog, as shown.

12. On the Toolbar, click **Sketch > Project/Include > Include 3D Geometry**.

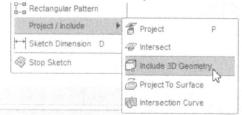

13. Select the YZ Plane.
14. Click the **Home** icon located at the top left corner of the ViewCube; the view orientation is changed to Home.
15. Click on the inner edge of the coil feature, as shown.

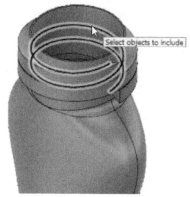

16. In the Browser, expand the Bodies folder and turn off the bulb icon next to the Body3.

17. Click **Stop Sketch** on the Toolbar.
18. Click **Create Sketch** on the **Sketch** panel.
19. Select the XY Plane.
20. On the **Navigation Bar**, click **Display Settings > Visual Style > Wireframe**.

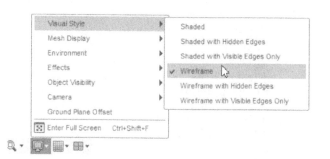

21. On the Toolbar, click **Sketch > Line**.
22. Click **Construction** on the Sketch Palette.
23. Zoom to the top portion of the model.
24. Create a horizontal construction line passing through the end point of the helical curve, as shown.

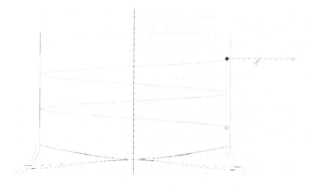

25. Deactivate the **Construction** icon on the **Sketch Palette**.
26. On the Toolbar, click **Sketch > Line**.
27. Create a closed profile, as shown.

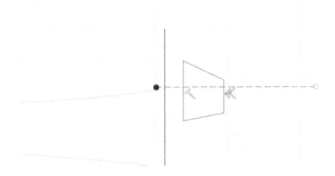

28. On the Toolbar, click **Sketch > Fillet** .
29. Select the two corners of the sketch, as shown.

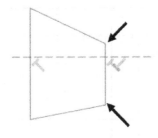

30. Type 0.04 in the **Fillet radius** box and press Enter.
31. Activate the **Sketch Dimension** tool and apply dimensions to the sketch, as shown.

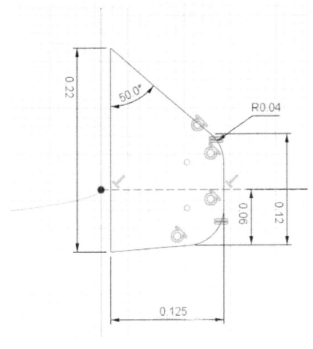

32. On the **Sketch Palette**, click **Constraints > Coincident**.
33. Select the vertical line of the sketch and the endpoint of the helical curve, as shown.

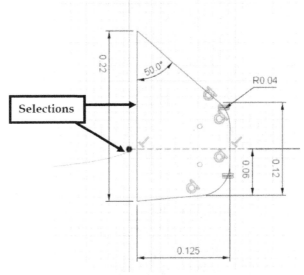

34. Click **Stop Sketch**.
35. Click the **Home** icon located at the top left corner of the ViewCube; the view orientation is changed to Home.
36. On the **Navigation Bar**, click **Display Settings > Visual Style > Shaded with Visible Edges Only.**
37. On the Toolbar, click **Create > Sweep.**

38. On the **Sweep** dialog, select **Type > Path + Guide Surface**.
39. Click in the region enclosed by the sketch.
40. Click the **Select** button next to the **Path** option.
41. Select the helical curve.
42. Click the **Select** button next to the **Guide Surface** option.
43. Select the inner face of the shell feature, as

shown.

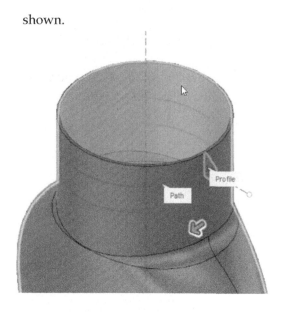

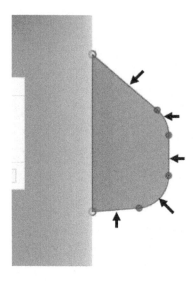

44. Select **Operation > Join**.
45. Click **OK** to create the sweep feature.

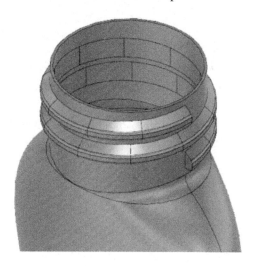

46. In the Browser, right click on the XY Plane, and then select **Create Sketch**.
47. On the Toolbar, click **Sketch > Project/Include > Project** .
48. Select the edges of the end face of the sweep feature.

49. Click **OK**.
50. Draw a straight line connecting the end points of the projected elements.

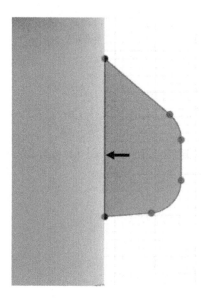

51. Click **Stop Sketch**.
52. Activate the **Revolve** tool and click in the region enclosed by the sketch.
53. Click the **Select** button next to the **Axis** option.
54. Select the vertical line of the sketch.
55. On the dialog, select **Type > Angle**, and then type-in **100** in the **Angle** box.
56. Select **Direction > One side**.
57. Select **Operation > Join**.

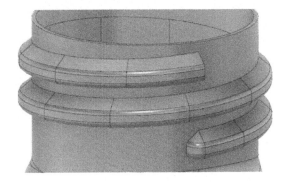

58. Click **OK**.
59. Likewise, blend the other end of the thread. Note that you need to enter a negative angle value.

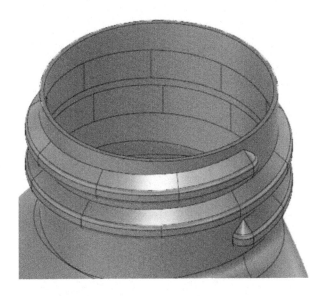

60. Save the model and close it.

# TUTORIAL 5

In this tutorial, you create a chair, as shown.

## Creating a 3D Sketch

1. On the Toolbar, click **Sketch > Create Sketch**.
2. Select the XZ Plane.
3. Click the **Home** icon located above the ViewCube. This changes the view orientation to Home.

4. On the Sketch Palette, check the **3D Sketch** option.
5. On the Toolbar, click **Sketch > Line**.
6. Select the origin point of the sketch.
7. Move the pointer along the X-axis (red line).
8. Type 12 and press Enter.

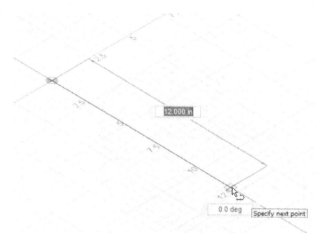

gizmo.

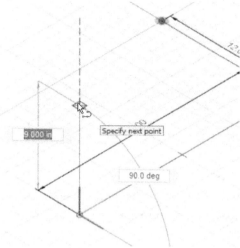

9.  On the Toolbar, click **Sketch > Line**.
10. Select the end point of the previous line.
11. Move the pointer in the Z-direction.
12. Type 20 and press Enter.

17. Type 18 and press Enter.

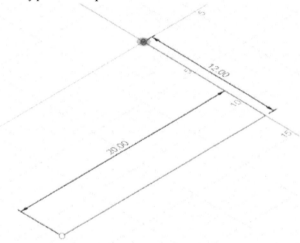

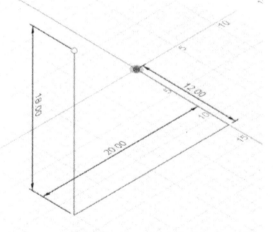

13. On the Toolbar, click **Sketch > Line**.
14. Select the end point of the previous line.
15. Move the pointer in the vertical direction; the 3D gizmo appears.

18. On the Toolbar, click **Sketch > Line**.
19. Select the end point of the vertical line.
20. Move the pointer along the Y-axis.
21. Type 22 and press Enter.

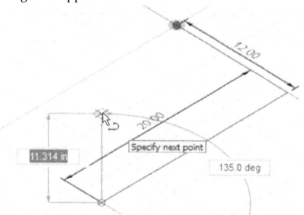

16. Move the pointer along the Z-axis of the 3D

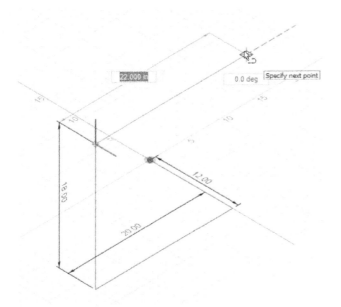

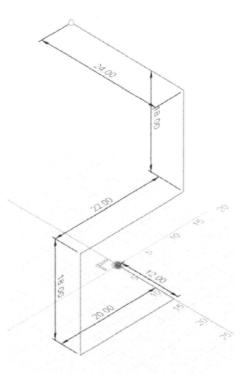

22. Activate the **Line** tool.
23. Select the endpoint of the previous line.
24. Move the pointer along the Z-axis.
25. Type 18 and press Enter.

30. Likewise, create the other lines, as shown.

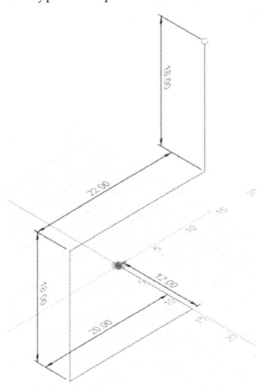

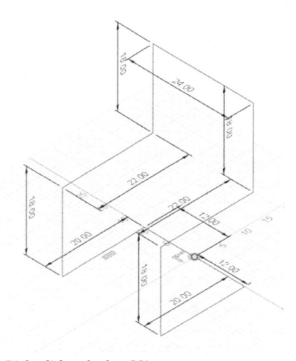

31. Right click and select **OK**.

32. On the Toolbar, click **Sketch > Fillet**       .

33. Select the corner point of the sketch, as shown.

26. Activate the **Line** tool.
27. Select the endpoint of the previous line.
28. Move the pointer along the X-axis.
29. Type 24 and press Enter.

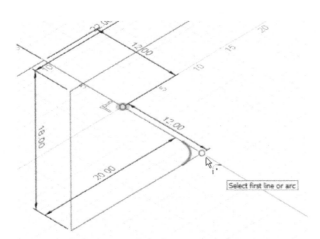

34. Type-in 3 in the **Fillet radius** box and press Enter on your keyboard.
35. Likewise, fillet the other corners, a shown.

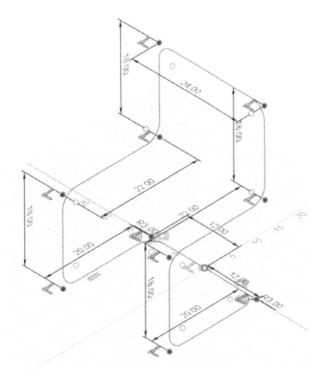

## Creating the Pipe feature

1. On the Toolbar, click **Create > Pipe**    .
2. Click on the sketch.
3. On the Pipe dialog, select **Section > Circular**.
4. Type-in 1.25 in the **Section Size** box.
5. Check the **Hollow** option.
6. Type-in 0.25 in the **Section Thickness** box.
7. Click **OK** to create the pipe feature.

8. On the Toolbar, click **Sketch > Sketch**.
9. Click on the YZ Plane.

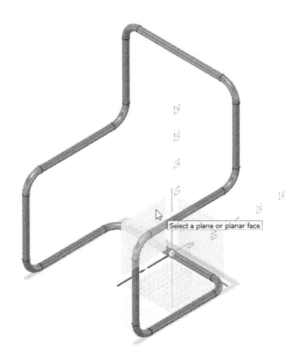

10. Check the **Slice** option on the Sketch Palette.

11. Draw the circles and dimension them, as shown.

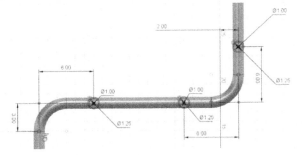

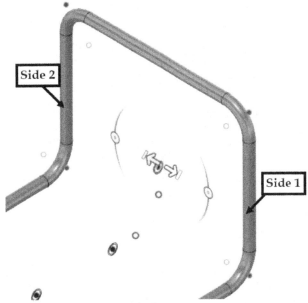

12. Click **Stop Sketch.**
13. Activate the **Extrude** tool and click in the outer loop of the sketch.

19. Select **Operation > Join**.
20. Click **OK** to extrude the sketch.

14. On the **Extrude** dialog, select **Direction > Two Sides**.
15. In the **Side 1** section, select **Extent > To Object**.
16. Select the right side of the pipe, as shown.
17. In the **Side 2** section, select **Extent > To Object**.
18. Select the left side of the pipe,

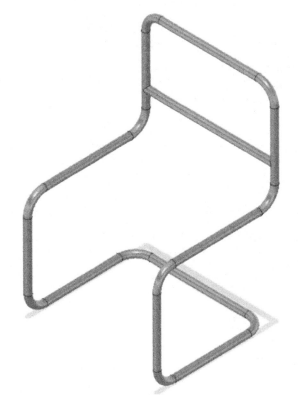

21. On the Browser, turn on the bulb icon next to the Sketch 2; the sketch is displayed.

22. Extrude the remaining loops, as shown.

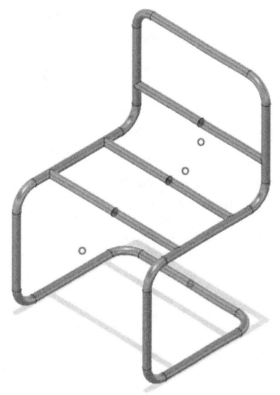

23. Hide the sketch.

## Creating the Freeform feature

1. On the Toolbar, click **Construct > Tangent Plane**.

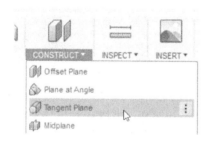

2. Select the cylindrical face, as shown.

3. In the **Browser**, expand the Origin folder, and then click the XZ Plane.
4. Click **OK** to create a plane tangent to the selected cylindrical face and parallel to the XZ plane.

5. Start a sketch on the new plane.

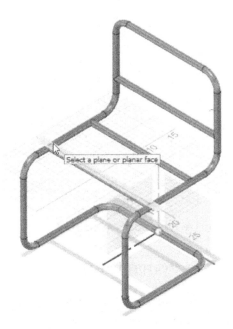

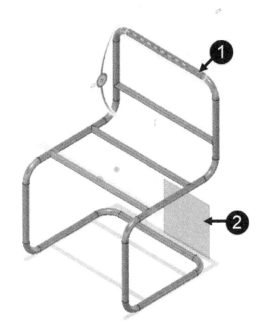

6. On the Toolbar, click **Sketch > Point**.
7. Place a point on the sketch plane and add dimension and constraint to position it.

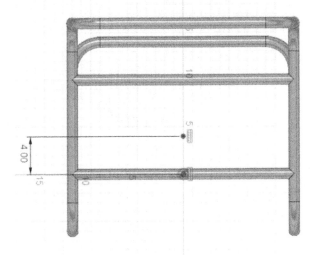

8. Click **Stop Sketch**.
9. On the Toolbar, click **Construct > Tangent Plane**.
10. Click on the vertical portion of the sweep feature to create a plane tangent to it.
11. In the Browser, click the XY Plane.

12. Click **OK**.
13. Start a sketch on the new plane.
14. Place a point and add dimension and constraint to it.

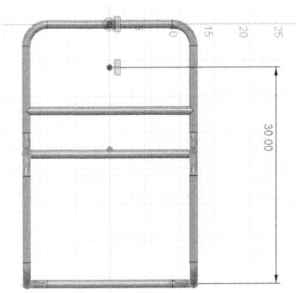

15. Click **Stop Sketch**.
16. Click the **Home** icon next to the ViewCube.
17. On the Toolbar, click **Create > Create Form**.
18. Click **OK** on the **Sculpt Environment** dialog.
19. In the Browser, expand the **Construction** folder, and then turn on the two tangent planes.

20. On the Toolbar, click **Create > Box**.
21. Select the plane tangent to the extruded feature.

22. On the **Box** dialog, click **Rectangle Type > Center**.
23. Select the sketch point to define the location of the freeform box.
24. Move the pointer outward and click.
25. On the Box dialog, type 28 in the **Length** box.
26. Type 19 on the **Width** box.
27. Type 4 in the Height box.
28. Type 4, 1 and 2 in the **Length Faces**, **Width Faces**, and **Height Faces** boxes, respectively.
29. Select **Symmetry > Mirror**.
30. Check the **Length Symmetry** option.
31. Click **OK** to create the freeform shape.

The symmetry line is displayed at the center.

## Editing the Freeform Shape

1. On the Toolbar, click **Modify > Edit Form**.
2. Click on the top face of the freeform shape.

3. Click on the arrow pointing upwards.
4. Drag it downwards 2 inches as shown in figure below.

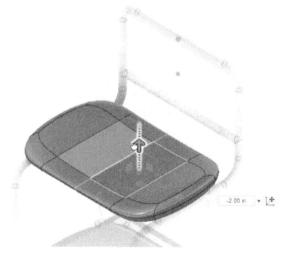

5. Click **OK** on the dialog.

6. On the Toolbar, click **Modify > Edit Form** 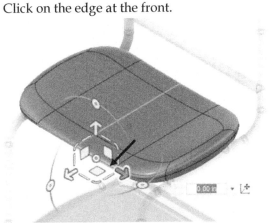.

7. Click on the edge at the front.

8. Drag the vertical arrow downwards.

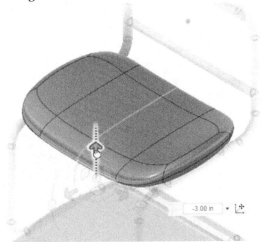

9. Click **OK** on the **Edit Form** dialog.

10. Activate the Freeform **Box** tool.

11. Select the tangent plane and click on the sketch point.

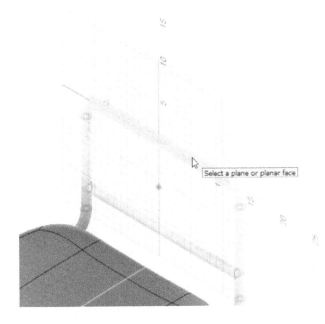

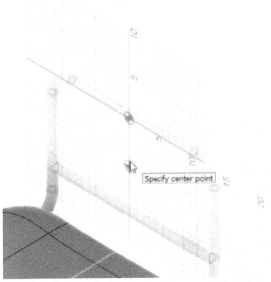

12. Move the pointer in the diagonal direction and click.

13. On the **Box** dialog, type-in 27, 16, and 3 in the **Length**, **Width**, and **Height** boxes, respectively.

14. Type **2** in the **Length Faces**, **Width Faces**, and **Height Faces** boxes, respectively

15. Click **OK**, and then click **Finish Freeform** on the Toolbar.

2. Click on the YZ Plane.
3. Click the origin point of the sketch to define the center point of the circle.
4. Move the pointer and type-in 0.75 in the box, and then press Enter twice.

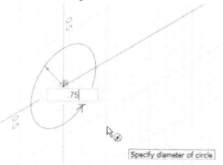

5. Type-in 3 in the **Height** box and press Enter.

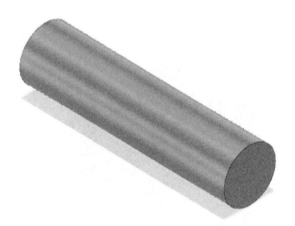

16. Save and close the file.

# TUTORIAL 6

In this tutorial, you create a bolt.

## Creating the second feature

1. Start a sketch on the YZ Plane.

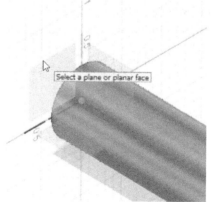

2. On the Toolbar, click **Sketch > Polygon** drop-down > **Inscribed Polygon** .

## Creating the Base Feature

1. On the Toolbar, click **Create > Cylinder** .

114

3. Click the sketch origin.

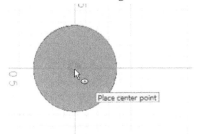

4. Type-in 6 in the **Edge Number** box.
5. Move the pointer vertically upward. You will notice that a dotted trace line appears between the origin point and the pointer.

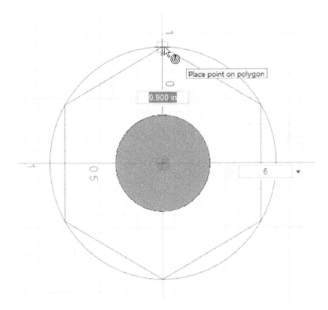

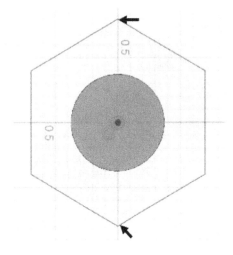

9. Activate the **Sketch Dimension** tool and create a dimension, as in figure.

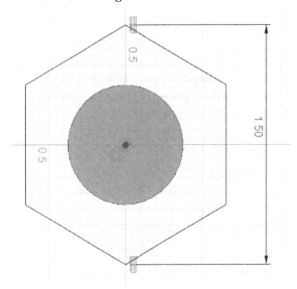

6. Click to create the polygon.
7. On the Sketch Palette, click **Constraints >**

   **Horizontal/Vertical** .
8. Select the vertices of the polygon, as shown.

10. Stop the sketch.
11. Activate the **Extrude** tool and click in the region enclosed by the sketch.
12. On the **Extrude** dialog, type-in -0.5 in the **Distance** box.
13. Select **Operation > Join**.
14. Click **OK**.

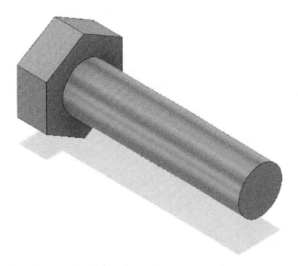

## Adding Threads

1.  On the Toolbar, click **Create > Thread** .
2.  Click on the cylindrical face of the model geometry.
3.  On the **Thread** dialog, uncheck the **Full Length** option and type-in **1.5** in the **Length** box.
4.  Check the **Modeled** option.
5.  Select **Thread Type > ANSI Unified Screw Threads**.
6.  Set **Size** to **0.75**.
7.  Select **Designation > 3/4 -10 UNC**.
8.  Select **Class > 2A**.
9.  Select **Direction > Right hand**.
10. Click **OK** to add the thread.

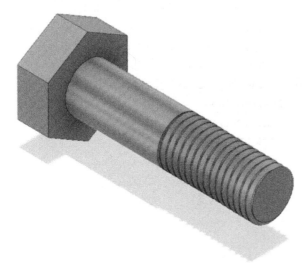

11. Save and close the file.

## TUTORIAL 7

In this tutorial, you create a plastic casing.

### Creating the First Feature

1.  Start Autodesk Fusion 360.
2.  On the Toolbar, click **Sketch > Create Sketch**.
3.  Select the XZ Plane.
4.  On the Toolbar, click **Sketch > Line**.
5.  Click in the second quadrant, move the cursor horizontally toward right, and then click to create a horizontal line, as shown.

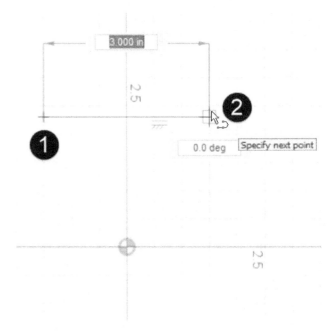

6.  On the Toolbar, click **Sketch > Arc drop-down > 3-Point Arc**.

7.  Select the right endpoint of the horizontal line.
8.  Move the cursor vertically downwards and click to define the second point.
9.  Move the pointer towards right and click on the horizontal axis line.

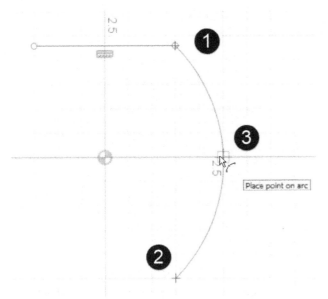

10. Likewise, create another three-point arc and horizontal line, as shown.

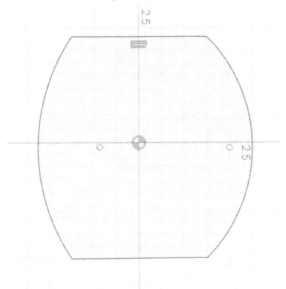

11. Create a vertical construction line from the origin point.

12. On the Sketch Palette, click **Constraints > Symmetry**.

13. Select the two arcs and the construction line.

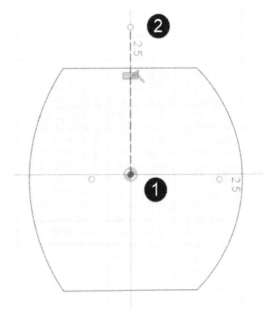

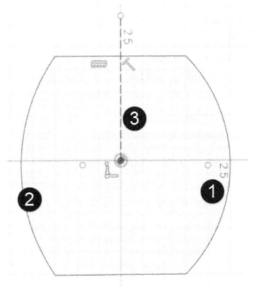

14. Likewise, create a horizontal construction line from the origin point, and then make the two horizontal lines symmetric about it.

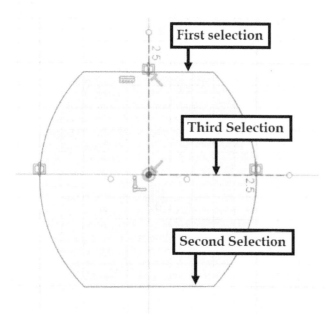

15. On the Sketch Palette, click **Constraints > Equal**.
16. Select the two horizontal lines.
17. On the Toolbar, click Sketch > Sketch Dimension.
18. Select anyone of the arcs and place the dimension.
19. Type 30 and press Enter.
20. Select the two horizontal lines and place the dimension.
21. Type 20 and press Enter.
22. Add dimension to the horizontal line.

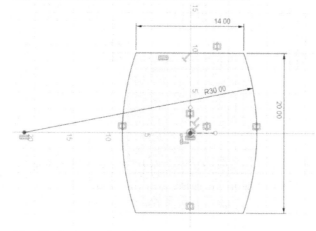

23. Click **Stop Sketch**.
24. Click **Create > Extrude** on the Toolbar; the **Extrude** dialog appears.
25. Click in the region enclosed by the sketch.
26. Set the **Distance** to 3.15.

27. Set the **Taper Angle** value to -10.
28. Click the **OK** button.

## Creating the Extruded surface

1. Click **Sketch > Create Sketch** on the Toolbar, and then select the YZ Plane.

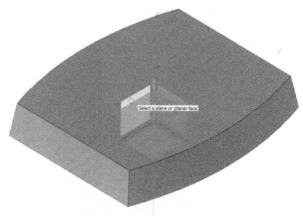

2. Check the **Slice** option on the Sketch Palette.

3. Click **Sketch > Spline > Fit Point Spline** on the Toolbar.

4. Create a spline, as shown in figure (See Chapter 5, Tutorial 4, Creating the First Section and Rails section).

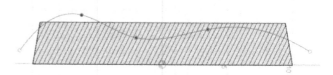

5. Apply dimensions to the spline, as shown below.

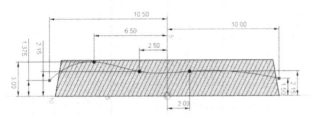

Adding dimension between two points of a spline locks the distance between the two points.

6.  Click **Stop Sketch**.
7.  On the Toolbar, click **Change Workspace > Patch**.

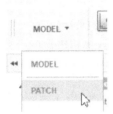

8.  On the Toolbar, click **Create > Extrude**.

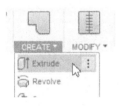

9.  Select the sketch.
32. Select **Direction > Symmetric**.
33. Set the **Measurement** to **Whole Length** ⊟.
34. Type 17 in the **Distance** box.
35. Select **Operation > New Body**.
36. Click **OK**.
37. On the Toolbar, click **Change Workspace > Model**.

## Replacing the top face of the model with the surface

1.  On the Toolbar, click **Modify > Replace Face**.

Now, you need to select the face to be replaced.

2.  Select the top face of the model.

Next, you need to select the target face or surface.

3.  Click the **Select** button next to the **Target Faces** option on the dialog.
4.  Select the extruded surface.
5.  Click **OK** to replace the top face with a surface.

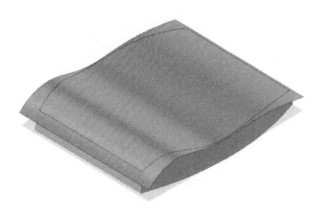

6. Hide the extruded surface by clicking the right mouse button on it, and then selecting **Show/Hide**.

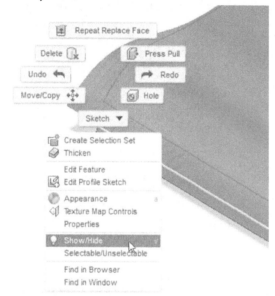

## Creating a fillet

1. On the Toolbar, click **Modify > Fillet**.
2. Click on the two edges of the model, as shown.

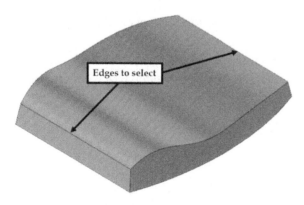

3. Select **Type > Constant Radius**.

4. Type **1.5** in the **Radius** box.
5. Click **OK**.

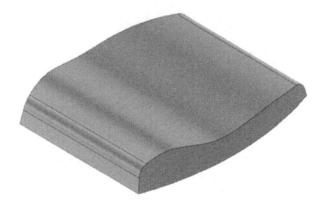

## Creating a Variable Radius fillet

1. On the Toolbar, click **Modify > Fillet**.
2. On the **Fillet** dialog, check the **Tangent Chain** option.
3. Select the curved edge on the model; the preview of the fillet appears.

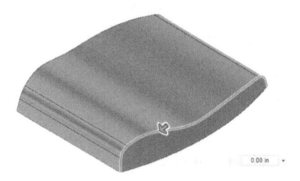

4. Select **Type > Variable Radius**.
5. Select a point on the fillet, as shown in figure.

6. Select another point the fillet, as shown in figure.

7. Click on the arrow displayed on the end point of the edge.
8. Type 0.6 in the **Radius** box.
9. Likewise, change the radius and position values at the other points, as shown.

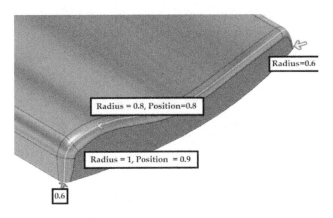

You can also specify the fillet continuity type.

7. Check the **Curvature (G2)** option.
8. Click **OK** to create the variable fillet.

9. Likewise, create another variable radius fillet on the other side.

## Shelling the Model

1. On the Toolbar, click **Modify > Shell**; the **Shell** dialog appears.
2. Select **Direction > Inside**.
3. Rotate the model and select the bottom face.
4. Type **0.2** in the **Inside Thickness** box.

5. Click **OK**.
6. Save and close the model.

# TUTORIAL 8

In this tutorial, you construct a patterned cylindrical shell.

## Constructing a cylindrical shell

1. Start Autodesk Fusion 360.
2. Create a sketch on the XZ plane, as shown.

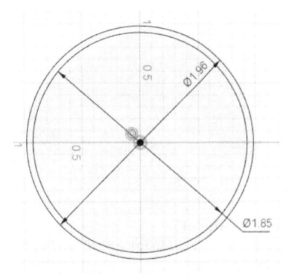

3.  Extrude the sketch up to 3.93 depth.

## Adding a Slot

1.  Activate the **Create Sketch** tool.
2.  Select the XY Plane.

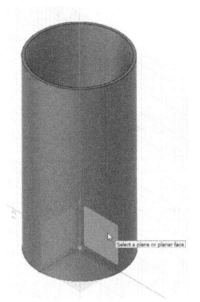

3.  Check the **Slice** option on the Sketch Palette. The model is sliced using the sketching plane.
4.  On the Toolbar, click **Sketch > Slot** drop-down **> Center to Center Slot**.

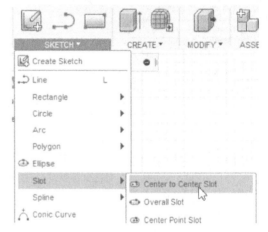

5.  Click to define the first point of the slot.
6.  Move the pointer up and click to define the second point.
7.  Move the pointer outward and click to create a slot.

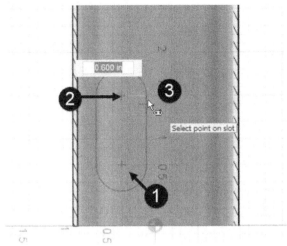

8. Apply the Vertical constraint between the Center point of the slot and the origin point.
9. Add dimensions to the slot.

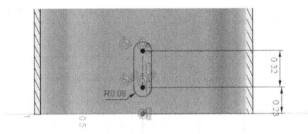

10. Click **Stop Sketch**.
11. Click the Home icon next to the ViewCube.
12. On the Toolbar, click **Create** panel > **Extrude**.
13. Click in the region enclosed by the sketch.
14. On the **Extrude** dialog, select **Extent > All**.
15. Make sure that the arrow on the extrude feature points in the forward direction.

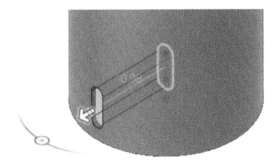

16. Select **Operation > Cut** from the dialog.
17. Click **OK**.

## Constructing the Rectangular pattern

1. On the Toolbar, click **Create > Pattern > Rectangular Pattern** ⬚.
2. On the **Rectangular Pattern** dialog, select **Pattern Type > Features**.
3. Click on the Extrude2 feature in the Timeline.

4. On the **Rectangular Pattern** dialog, click the **Select** button next to the **Directions** option.
5. Select the Y Axis from the coordinate system.

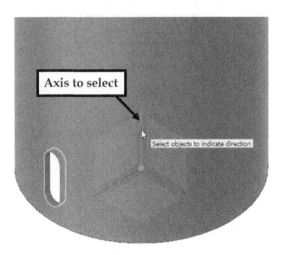

6. On the dialog, select the **Spacing** option from the **Distance Type** drop-down.
7. Type **6** in the **Quantity** box.
8. Type **0.629** in the **Distance** box.
9. Click **OK**.

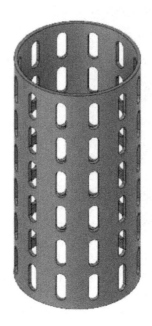

## Constructing the Circular pattern

1. On the Toolbar, click **Create > Pattern >**
   **Circular Pattern** .

2. On the **Circular Pattern** dialog, select **Pattern**
   **Type > Features**.

3. In the timeline, click on the **R-Pattern1** and the
   **Extrude2** features.

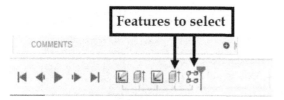

4. On the **Circular Pattern** dialog, click the **Select**
   button next to the **Axis** option and select the
   cylindrical face of the model.

5. Select **Type > Full**.

6. Type-in **12** in the **Quantity** box.

7. Click **OK** to make the circular pattern.

11. Save and close the model.

# Chapter 7: Top-Down Assembly and Joints

In this chapter, you will learn to

- Create a top-down assembly
- Create assembly joints

## TUTORIAL 1

In this tutorial, you will create the model shown in figure. You use top-down assembly approach to create this model.

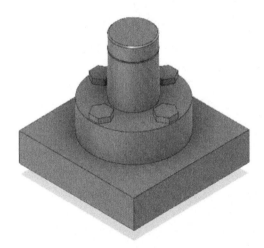

### Creating a component in the Assembly

In a top-down assembly approach, you create components of an assembly directly in the assembly by using the **Create** tool.

1. Click the **Save** icon on the Application Bar.
2. Type **Ch7_tut1** in the **Name** box on the **Save** dialog.
3. Click **Save**.

4. Click **New Component** on the **Assemble** panel of the Toolbar. The **New Component** dialog appears.

5. Select the **Empty Component** option.
6. Enter **Base** in the **Name** field.
7. Check the **Activate** option.
8. Click **OK**.
9. Click **Sketch > Create Sketch** on the Toolbar.
10. Select **XZ Plane**.
11. Create a sketch as shown below.

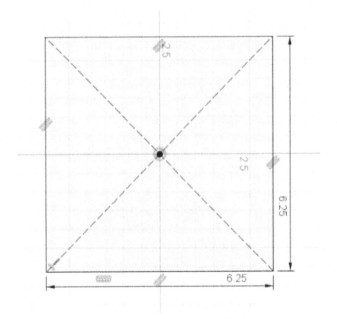

12. Click **Stop Sketch**.
13. Click **Create > Extrude** on the Toolbar and extrude the sketch up to 1.5 in.

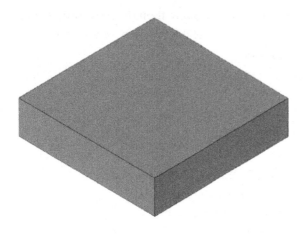

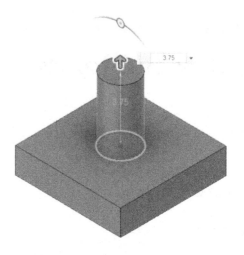

14. Start a sketch on the top face and draw a circle of **2** in diameter.

17. Create a counterbore hole on the second feature (See Chapter 6, Tutorial 1, Create a Counterbore Hole section). The following figure shows the dimensions of the counterbore hole.

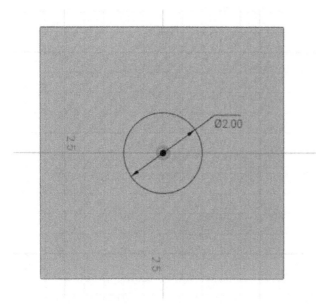

15. Click **Stop Sketch**
16. Extrude the sketch up to 3.75 in distance.

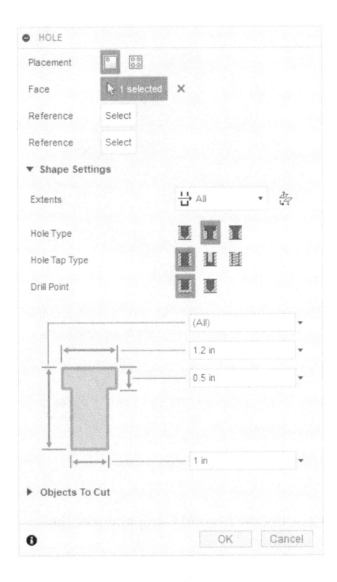

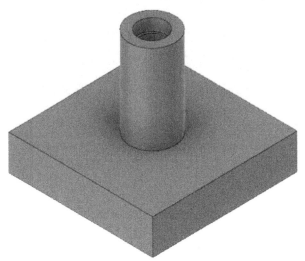

18. Start a new sketch on the top face of the first feature.

19. Create a 3.5 diameter circle with the **Construction** button pressed on the Sketch Palette.

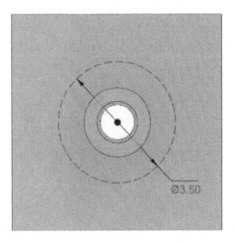

20. On the Toolbar, click **Sketch > Point**.
21. Place a point on the circle.
22. On the Sketch Palette, click **Constraints > Horizontal/Vertical**.
23. Select the sketch origin and the point.

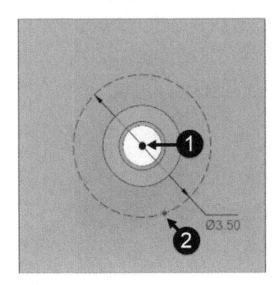

24. Click **Stop Sketch**.
25. On the Toolbar, click **Create > Hole**.
26. Select the sketch point.
27. On the **Hole** dialog, specify the settings, as shown.

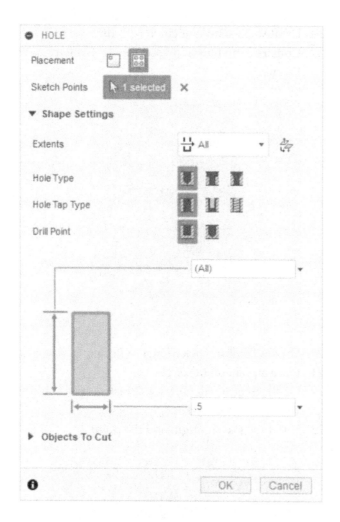

28. Click **OK** to create the hole.

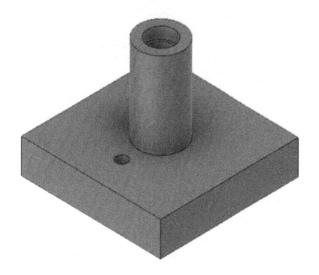

29. Create a circular pattern of the hole (See Chapter 6, Tutorial 1, Create a Circular Pattern).

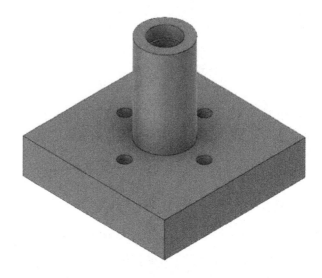

30. In the Browser, right click on Ch7_tut1, and then select Activate; the assembly is activated.

## Creating the Second Component of the Assembly

1. Click **Assemble > New Component** on the Toolbar; the **New Component** dialog appears.
2. Enter **Spacer** in the **Name** field.
3. Check the **Activate** option.
4. Click **OK**.
5. Click **Sketch > Create Sketch** on the Toolbar.
6. Select the top face of the Base.

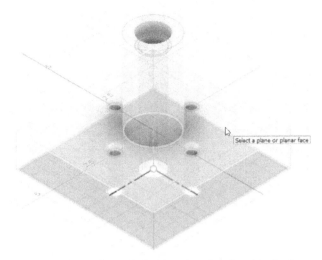

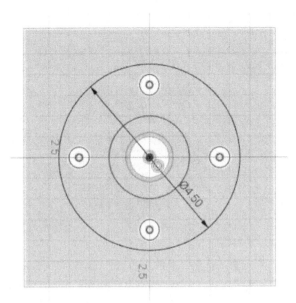

7.  On the Toolbar, click **Sketch > Project/Include > Project** and select the circular edges of the Base.

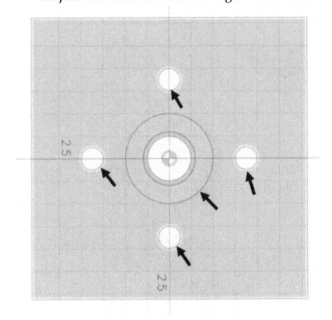

10. Click **Stop Sketch**.
11. Extrude the sketch up to 1.5 in.

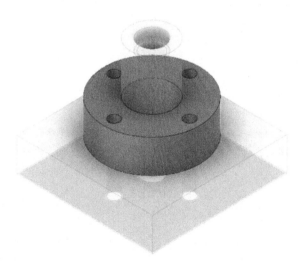

8.  Click **OK**.
9.  Draw a circle of 4.5 in diameter.

12. In the Browser, right click on Ch7_tut1 and select **Activate**.

## Creating the third Component of the Assembly

1.  Click **Assemble > New Component** on the Toolbar; the **New Component** dialog appears.
2.  Enter **Shoulder Screw** in the **Name** field.
3.  Check **Activate** option.
4.  Click **OK**.
5.  Start a sketch on the YZ Plane.

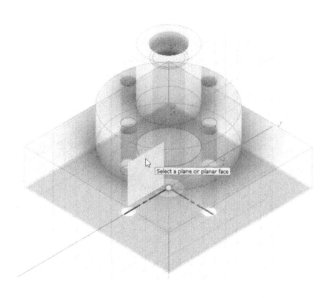

6. Draw a sketch, as shown in figure.

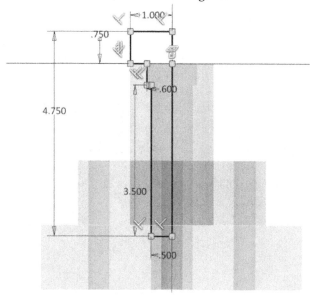

7. Click **Stop Sketch**.
8. Activate the **Revolve** tool and revolve the sketch.

9. On the Toolbar, click **Modify > Chamfer**.

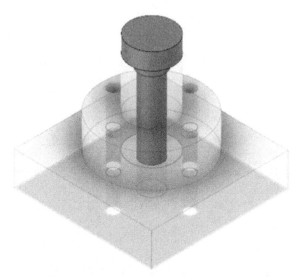

10. Chamfer the edges, as shown in figure. The Chamfer **Distance** is 0.06 in.

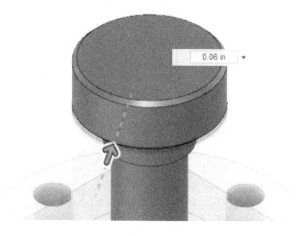

11. Activate the **Fillet** tool and fillet the edges, as shown in figure. The fillet radius is 0.02 in.

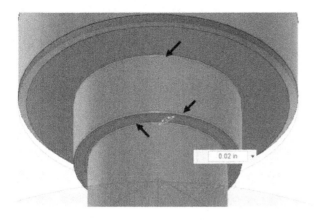

12. Right-click on Ch7_tut1 in the Browser, and then select **Activate**.

## Create the Bolt

1. On the Toolbar, click **Assemble > New Component**.
2. On the **New Component** dialog, select the **Empty Component** option.
3. Type **Bolt** in the **Name** box.
4. Select the **Activate** option.
5. Click **OK**.
6. On the Toolbar, click **Sketch > Create Sketch**.
7. Click on the top face of the spacer.
8. On the Toolbar, click **Sketch > Project/Include > Project**.
9. Click on the hole edge.

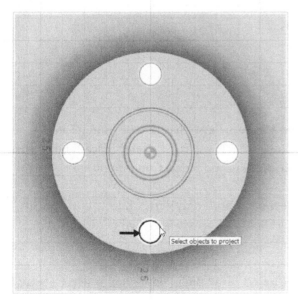

10. Click **OK**.
11. Click **Stop Sketch**.

12. On the Toolbar, click **Create > Extrude**.
13. Click in the region enclosed by the sketch.
14. Type -3.5 in the **Distance** box and click **OK**.

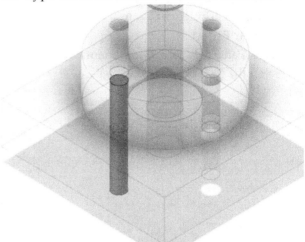

15. On the Toolbar, click **Sketch > Create Sketch**.
16. Click on the top face of the extruded feature.
17. Create a polygon, as shown in figure.

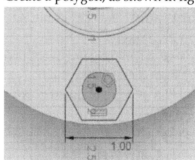

18. Click **Stop Sketch**.
19. Extrude the sketch up to 0.25 in distance.

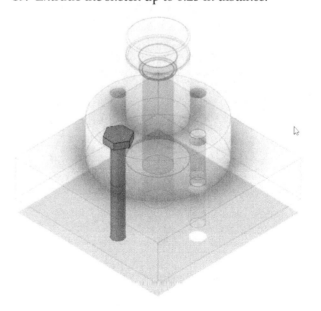

20. Activate the assembly.

## Patterning components in an assembly

1. On the Toolbar, click **Create > Pattern > Circular Pattern**.
2. Select **Pattern Type > Components**.
3. Select the **Bolt** from the Browser.

4. On the **Circular Pattern** dialog, click the **Select** button next to the **Axis** option.
5. Click on the large cylindrical face of the Spacer to define the axis of the circular pattern.
6. On the dialog, type-in 4 in the **Quantity** box
7. Select **Type > Full**.
8. Click **OK** to pattern the bolt.

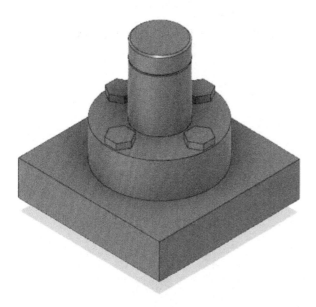

## Creating a Rigid Group

1. In the Browser, right click on the **Base**

component, and then select **Ground**.

2. On the Toolbar, click **Assemble > Rigid Group**.

3. Select all the components one-by-one.
4. Click **OK** to create the rigid group.

## Using the Measure tool

The **Measure** tool helps you to measure the size and position of the model. You can measure the various parameters of the model such as length, angle, radius, and so on.

1. On the Toolbar, click **Inspect > Measure** ![measure icon] ; the **Measure** dialog appears on the screen.

The **Measure** dialog has three selection filters (shown from left to right): **Select Face/Edge/Vertex**, **Select Body**, and **Select Component**.

The **Select Face/Edge/Vertex** filter allows you to select only the faces, edges, and vertices of the model.

The **Select Body** filter allows you to select a body for measurement.

The **Select Component** filter allows you to select the part geometry and assemblies.

2. Click the **Select Face/Edge/Vertex** filter, and then select the linear edge, as shown.

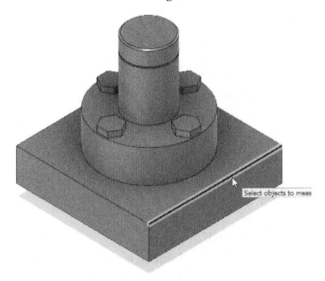

The length of the selected edge is displayed on the **Measure** dialog.

3. Select the cylindrical face, as shown; the Measure window displays results.

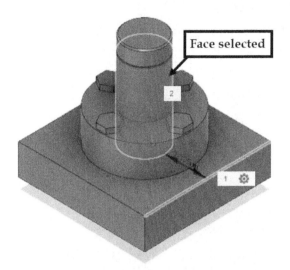

The **Measure** dialog displays the results of the first and second selections separately. In addition to that, the distance between the two selected entities is displayed.

4. Close the **Measure** dialog.
5. Save and close the assembly and its parts.

# TUTORIAL 2

In this tutorial, you create a slider crank mechanism by applying Joints.

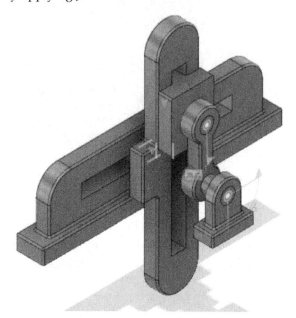

1. Create the **Slider Crank Assembly** folder inside the project folder.
2. Download the part files of the assembly by reaching us at online.books999@gmail.com.
3. Click the **Show Data Panel** icon on the top left corner of the window.
4. Click the **Upload** button on the **Data** panel.
5. On the **Upload** dialog, set the Location to **Autodesk Fusion 360 Basics Tutorial > master > Slider Crank Assembly**.
6. Click the **Select Files** button.
7. Next, save the files in the **Slider Crank Assembly** folder.
8. Start a new assembly file.

## Inserting the Components into the Design

1. On the Application Bar, click the **Save** icon.
2. Type **Slider Crank Assembly** in the **Name** box on the **Save** dialog.
3. Click **Save**.
4. To insert the base component, click the **Show Data Panel** icon.
5. Right click on the Base file in the **Data** panel, and then select **Insert into Current Design**.
6. Click **OK**.

7. In the Browser, right click on the Base component, and then select **Ground**.
8. Insert the remaining components into the design.

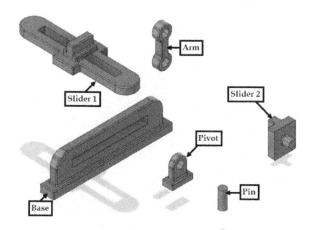

## Creating the Slider Joint

1. Click **Assemble > Joint** on the Toolbar; the **Joint** dialog appears.

2. Set the **Type** to **Slider**.

3. Select the face on the Slider1, as shown below.

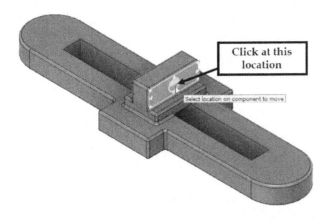

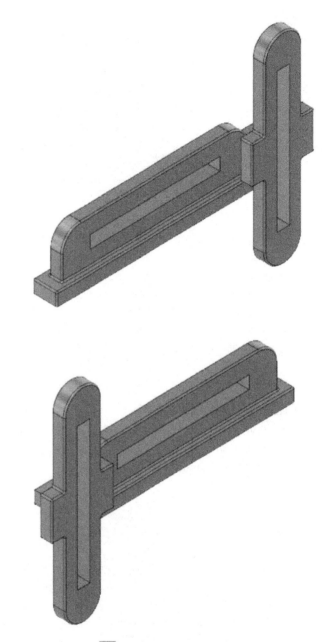

4. Select the face on the Base, as shown below; the two faces are aligned.

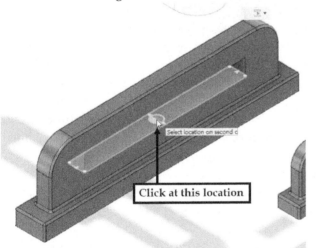

5. On the dialog, select **Slide > Y Axis**.
6. Type 90 in the **Angle** box.
7. Click the **Animate** ▶ icon; the slider slides along the slot.

8. Click the **Stop** ■ icon.
9. Click **OK**.

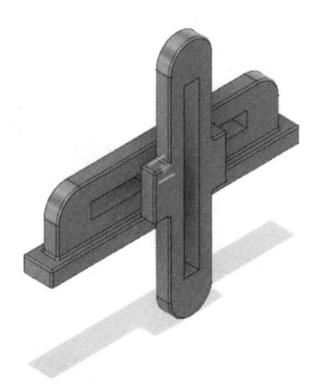

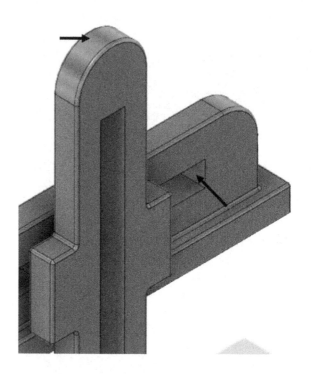

## Editing the Joint Limits

You have noticed that the slider slides beyond the base component. You need to restrict the motion of the slider between the two faces, as shown.

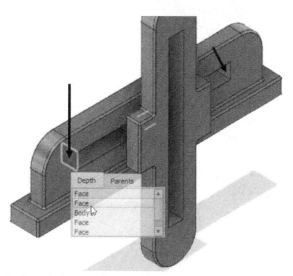

Before defining the joint limits, you need to know the distance between the center of the Slider 1 and anyone of the limiting faces

1. On the Toolbar, click **Inspect > Measure**.
2. Select the two faces, as shown.

3. In the Measure dialog, click on the **Minimum Distance** value in the **Results** section; the value is copied to the clipboard.

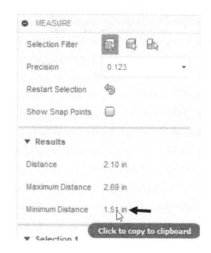

4. Close the **Measure** dialog.
5. In the Browser, expand the Joints folder, right click on the **Slider 1** joint, and then select **Edit Joint Limits**.

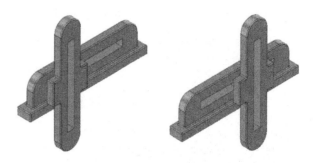

6. Check the **Maximum** option.
7. Select the value in the **Maximum** box.
8. Press Ctrl+V to paste the maximum distance value in the box.
9. Check the **Minimum** box.
10. Type -1.51 in the **Minimum** box.

## Creating Second Slider Joint

1. Click the corner of the ViewCube, as shown; the orientation of the design is changed.

2. Click **Assemble > Joint** on the Toolbar.
3. On the dialog, set the **Type** to **Slider** .
4. Select the face on the Slider2, as shown below.

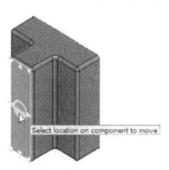

5. Select the right edge of the top face of the ViewCube; the orientation of the design changes.

6. Click the **Fit** icon on the Navigation Bar
7. Select the face on the Slider1, as shown below.
8. On the dialog, select **Slide > X Axis**.
9. Click **OK**.

11. Click **OK**.
12. Right click on the Slider 1 joint in the Browser, and then select **Animate Joint**; the slider joint is animated. Notice that the slider moves between the end faces of the Base component.
13. Press Esc to stop the animation.

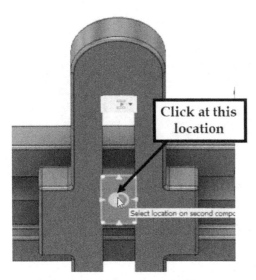

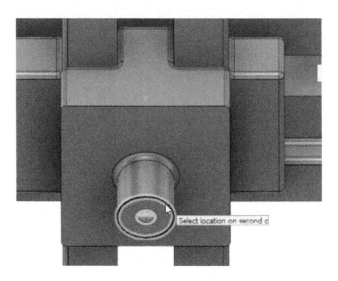

## Creating the Revolute Joint

1. Click **Assemble > Joint** on the Toolbar.
2. Set **Type** to **Revolute**.

3. Select the circular edge of the arm, as shown below.

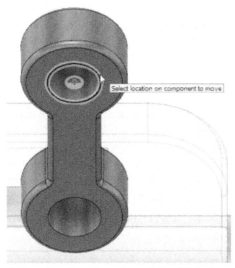

4. Select the circular edge of the Slider2.

2. Select **Rotate > Z Axis**.
3. Click **OK.**

## Creating the Rigid Joint

1. Click the **Home** icon next to the ViewCube.
2. Click on the cylindrical face of the Arm and drag it towards left; the arm is revolved.

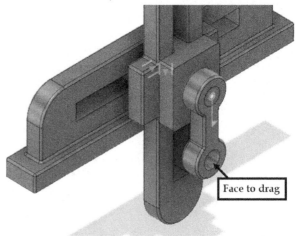

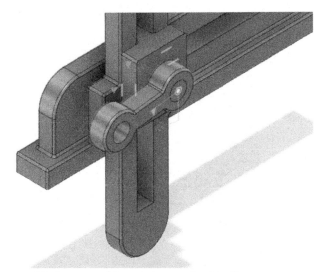

3. Click **Assemble > Joint** on the Toolbar.
4. Click the **Capture Position** button on the **Fusion 360** dialog.

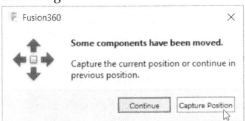

5. Set the **Type** to **Rigid** .
6. Select the top face on the pin.

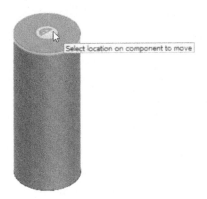

7. Click on the corner point of the ViewCube, as shown.

8. Select the cylindrical face of the arm.

9. Click **OK**.

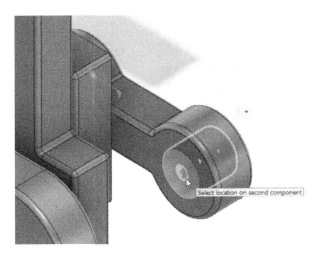

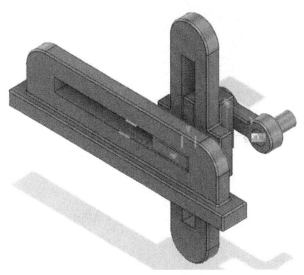

## Adding more assembly joints

1. Create another revolute joint between the Pin and the Pivot.

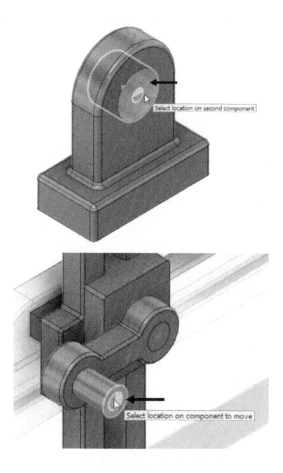

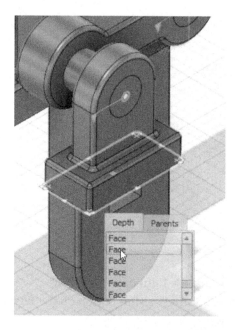

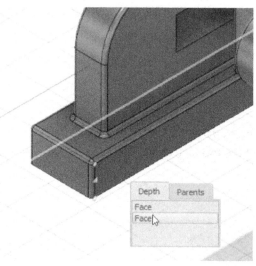

Next, you need to fix the Pivot.

2.  On the Toolbar, click **Modify > Align**.

3.  On the **Align** dialog, select **Object > Component**.
4.  Select the bottom faces of the Pivot and Base.

5.  Check the **Capture Position** option.
6.  Click **OK**.
7.  On the **Align** dialog, select **Object > Component**.
8.  In the Browser, expand the **Origin** folder and select the XY plane.

then select the two Revolute joints.

9. In the Browser, expand the Pivot folder, and then expand the Origin folder under it.

10. Select the XY Plan of the Pivot.

11. Check the **Capture Position** option, and then click **OK**.

12. In the Browser, right click on the Pivot component, and then select Ground; the component is grounded.

## Creating Motion Links

1. On the Toolbar, click **Assemble > Motion Link**.

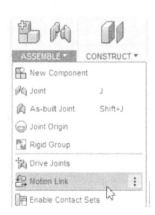

2. Click **Capture Position**.

3. Expand the **Joints** folder in the Browser, and

4. Check the **Reverse** option.

5. Click **OK**.

6. Right click on anyone of the Revolute joint, and then select **Animate Model**; the model is animated.

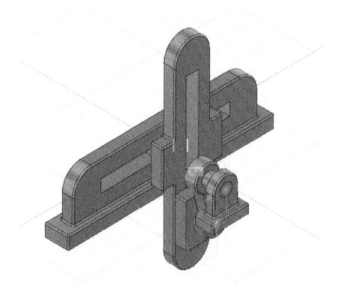

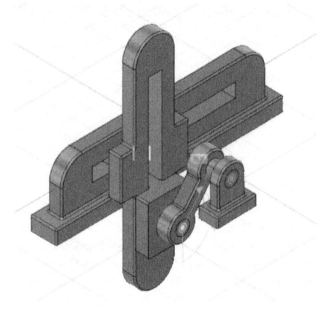

7. Press Esc to stop the animation.
8. Save and close the assembly.

# Chapter 8: Dimensions and Annotations

In this chapter, you will learn to

- Create Centerlines and Centered Pattern
- Edit Hatch Pattern
- Apply Dimensions
- Place Hole callouts
- Place Leader Text
- Place Datum Feature
- Place Feature control frame
- Place Surface texture symbol
- Modify the Title Block Information

## TUTORIAL 1

In this tutorial, you create the drawing shown below.

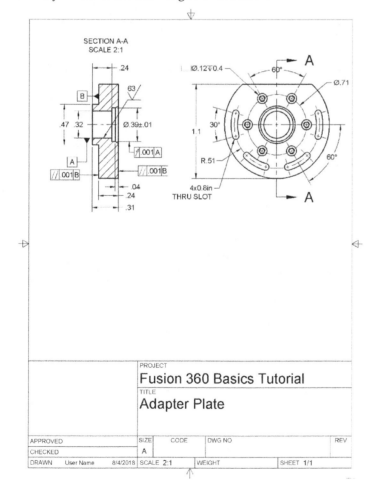

## Starting a New Drawing File

1. Click on the **Show Data Panel** icon on the Application Bar.
2. On the **Data** panel, double-click on the **Ch6_tut1** file to open it.
3. Close the **Data** panel.
4. To start a new drawing, click the **File > New Drawing > From Design** on the Application Bar.

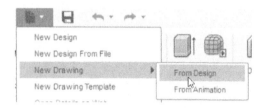

5. On the **Create Drawing** dialog, uncheck the **Full Assembly** option.
6. Select the body from the graphics window.
7. Select **Template > From Scratch**.
8. Select **Standard > ASME**.
9. Select **Units > in**.
10. Select **Sheet Size > A (8.5in x 11in)**.
11. Click **OK**.
12. Set the **Scale** to 2:1.
13. Select **Orientation > Front**.
14. Set the **Style** to **Visible Edges**.
15. Place the view on the right-side on the drawing sheet.

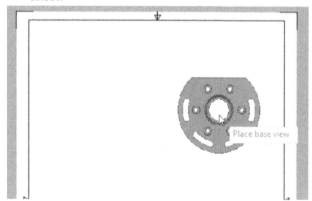

16. Click **OK**.
17. Click **Drawing Views > Section View** on the Toolbar.
18. Select the front view.
19. Draw the section line on the front view.

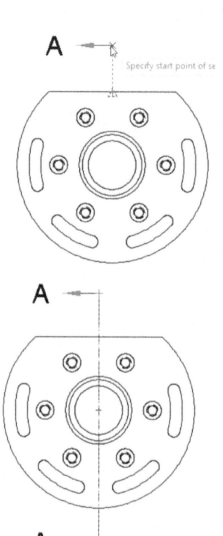

13. Right-click and select **Continue**.
14. Place the section view on the left side.
15. Click **OK**.

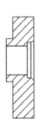
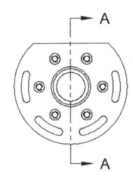

SECTION A-A
SCALE 2:1

## Creating Centerlines and Centered Patterns

1. Click **Geometry > Centerline** on the Toolbar.

2. Select the parallel lines on the section view, as shown below; the centerline is created.

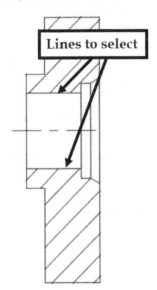

3. Right click and select **OK**.
4. Click **Geometry > Center Mark** on the Toolbar.

5. Select the circle located at the center.

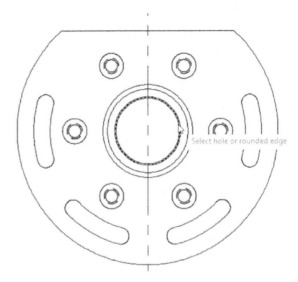

6. On the Toolbar, click **Geometry > Center Mark Pattern** .
7. Select the center point of anyone of the counterbored holes.

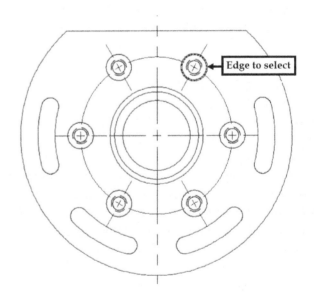

8. Check the **Auto-complete** and **Full PCD** options.
9. Click **OK**.
10. Likewise, create another centered pattern on the curved slots.
11. Make sure that the **Full PCD** option is unchecked. Click **OK**.

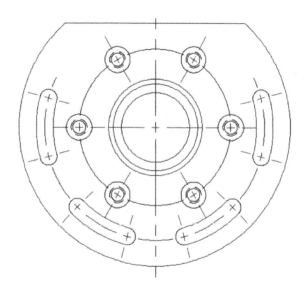

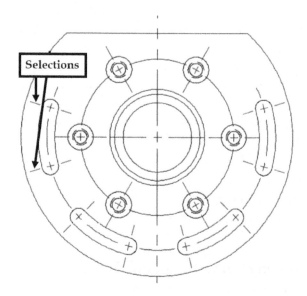

## Editing the Hatch Pattern

1.  Double-click on the hatch pattern of the section view; the **Hatch** dialog appears.

You can select the required hatch pattern from the **Pattern** drop-down. Use the **Scale** box to change the distance between the hatch lines. Type-in a value in the **Angle** box to the change the angle of the hatch lines.

2.  Click **Close**.

## Applying Dimensions

1.  Click **Dimensions > Dimension** on the Toolbar.
2.  Select the centerlines of the slot, as shown.

3.  Move the pointer toward left and click.

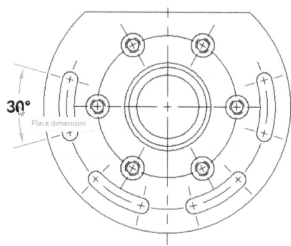

4.  Create angular dimensions between the holes, and then between slots. To create the angular dimension between the slots, you need to create the angular dimension between the bolt circles.

146

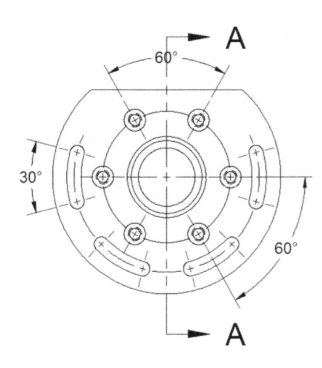

5. Dimension the pitch circle radius of the slots.

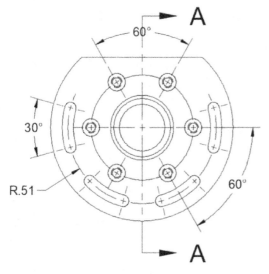

6. With the **Dimension** tool active, select the horizontal line of the front view.
7. Right click and select **Quadrant**.
8. Select the lower quadrant point of the view.

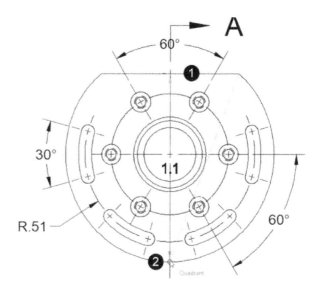

9. Place the dimension on the left side.

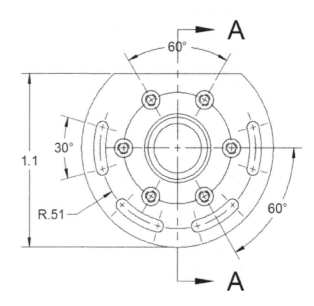

10. Activate the **Dimension** tool.
11. Select the counterbore hole and place the dimension, as shown below.

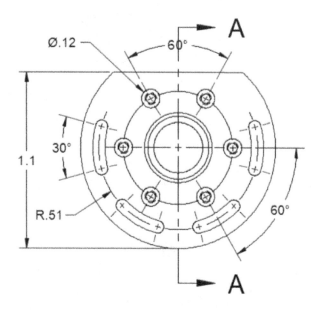

12. Right click and select **OK**.
13. Double click on the diameter dimension.
14. Click before the dimension value.

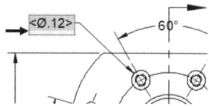

15. On the **Dimension** dialog, select **Insert Symbol > Counterbore**.
16. Click after the dimension value.

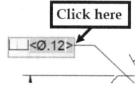

17. Select **Insert Symbol > Depth**.
18. Type **0.4** and click **Close** on the **Dimension** dialog.

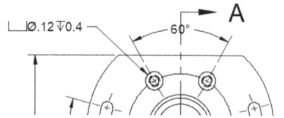

19. Add a pitch circle diameter to the counterbore holes.

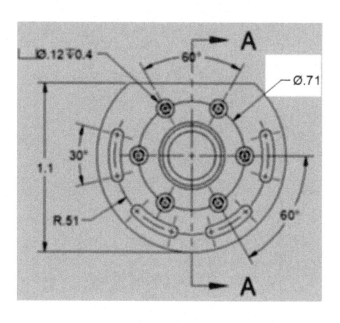

20. Click **Text > Leader** on the Toolbar.

21. Select the slot end, as shown below.

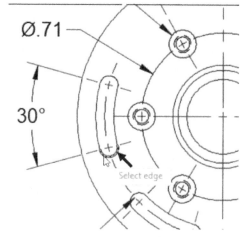

22. Move the cursor away and click.
23. Enter the text shown below.

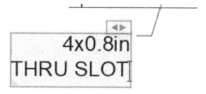

24. Click **Close**.

25. Double-click on the section label below the section view.
26. Select all the text.
27. On the **Text** dialog, set the **Height** to **0.12 in**. Click **Close**.
28. Click on the section label.
29. Select the square grip, move the pointer upward, and then place the label at the top.

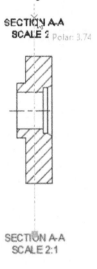

30. Click **Dimension** on the **Dimensions** panel.
31. Select the endpoints of the lines, as shown below.

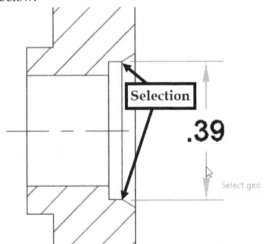

32. Move the pointer toward right and click to place the dimension.
33. Right click and select **OK**.
34. Double click on the dimension.
35. Click before the dimension.
36. On the **Dimension** dialog, select **Insert Symbol > Diameter**.

37. On the dialog, expand the **Tolerance** section.
38. Select **Type > Symmetrical**.
39. Set the **Tolerance** value to **0.01**.
40. Click **Close**.

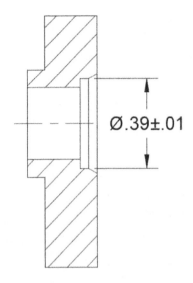

41. Likewise, create the other dimensions, as shown below.

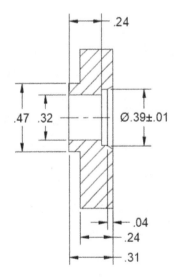

### Placing the Datum Identifier

1. Click **Symbols > Datum Identifier** on the Toolbar.

2. Select the edge of the section view, as shown below.

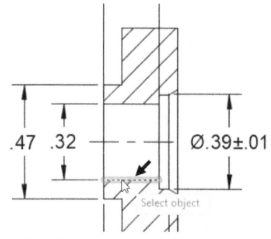

3. Move the cursor toward left and click.
4. Move the cursor downward and click.
5. Move the cursor toward left and click; the **Datum Identifier** dialog appears. Make sure that A is entered in the dialog.
6. Click **OK**.

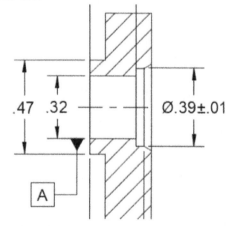

7. Likewise, place a datum feature B, as shown below.

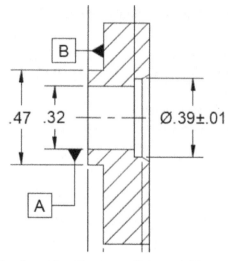

## Placing the Feature Control Frame

1. Click **Symbols > Feature Control Frame** on the Toolbar.

2. Select the edge, as shown below.

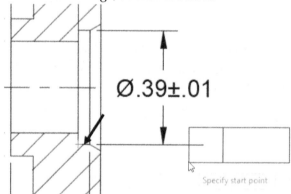

3. Move the cursor horizontally toward right and click.
4. Move the cursor downward and click to specify the location.
5. Right click and select **Continue**.
6. On the **Feature Control Frame** dialog, select the **Circular Runout** symbol from the **Geometric Symbol** section.

**Dimensions and Annotations**

7. Enter 0.001 in the **First Tolerance** box and **A** in the **First Datum** box.
8. Click **OK**.

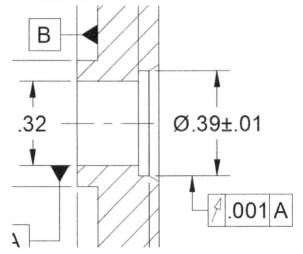

## Placing the Surface Texture Symbols

1. Click **Symbols > Surface Texture** on the Toolbar.

2. Click on the inner cylindrical face of the hole, as shown below.

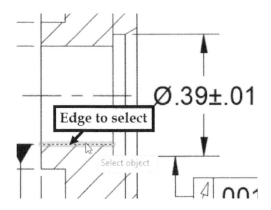

3. Specify the start point on the selected edge.
4. Move the pointer diagonally toward right, and then click specify the location of the symbol.

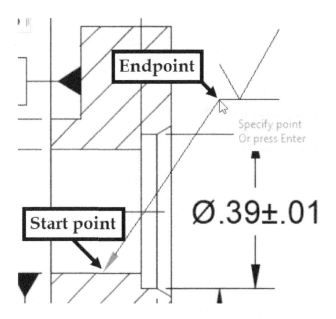

5. Right-click and select **Continue**; the **Surface Texture** dialog appears.
6. Set the **Roughness Max** value to 63.
7. Click **OK**.

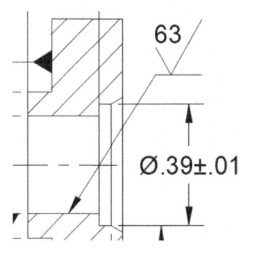

8. Apply the other annotations of the drawing.

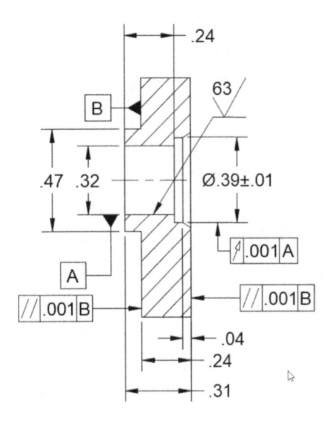

## Modifying the Title Block Information

1. Double click on the title block; the Title Block dialog appears.
2. Enter the information, as shown next.

3. Click **OK**.
4. Save the file.
5. To export the file to AutoCAD format, click **Output > Output DWG**.

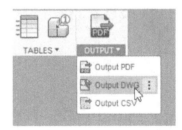

6. Click **Save**.
7. Close the file.